The Queen of the Hearth

CLASSICS OF IRISH HISTORY
General Editor: Tom Garvin

Original publication dates of reprinted titles are given in brackets

The Queen of the Hearth

✦

FATHER PATRICK DINNEEN

With an introduction and notes
by Philip O'Leary

UNIVERSITY COLLEGE DUBLIN PRESS
Preas Choláiste Ollscoile Bhaile Átha Cliath

First published in 2013 by University College Dublin Press

© Philip O'Leary 2013

ISBN 978-1-906359-72-0
ISSN 1393-6883

University College Dublin Press
Newman House, 86 St Stephen's Green
Dublin 2, Ireland
www.ucdpress.ie

Cataloguing in Publication data available
from the British Library

Typeset in Ehrhardt by Ryan Shiels, Scotland
Text design by Lyn Davies,
Frome, Somerset, England
Printed on acid-free paper by
Antony Rowe, Chippenham, Wilts.

The Queen of the Hearth

✦

FATHER PATRICK DINNEEN

With an introduction and notes
by Philip O'Leary

UNIVERSITY COLLEGE DUBLIN PRESS
Preas Choláiste Ollscoile Bhaile Átha Cliath

First published in 2013 by University College Dublin Press

© Philip O'Leary 2013

ISBN 978-1-906359-72-0
ISSN 1393-6883

University College Dublin Press
Newman House, 86 St Stephen's Green
Dublin 2, Ireland
www.ucdpress.ie

Cataloguing in Publication data available
from the British Library

Typeset in Ehrhardt by Ryan Shiels, Scotland
Text design by Lyn Davies,
Frome, Somerset, England
Printed on acid-free paper by
Antony Rowe, Chippenham, Wilts.

CONTENTS

CONTENTS

INTRODUCTION

Philip O'Leary

In his 1910 book *The Pope's Green Island*, W. P. Ryan devoted a chapter to what he called 'The Fear of Liberal Catholicism', claiming that the Irish intellectual most afflicted with this phobia was Father Patrick Dinneen (An tAthair Pádraig Ó Duinnín), 'one of our foremost Irish writers and a remarkable individuality in every way.'[1] He went on to develop this picture:

> He is a very composite individuality, and, like many great men, has what ordinary vision regards as peculiarities. We might liken him to the mountain stream: now radiant in its gleam, now unaccountable in its course, at times eddying vehemently round obstacles, anon noble in its volume and its force. He has intense convictions, and a host of minor opinions that seem incidental and unimportant, but for which he is prepared to do battle with fiery ardour.[2]

Ryan's emphasis in this chapter was on Dinneen as 'a perfervid champion of ecclesiasticism' who saw 'enmity and danger to the Church in the straight and strong assertion of the rights of laymen'.[3] But by no means was Dinneen's 'fiery ardour' limited to issues explicitly ecclesiastic. He was, at the very least, wary of most manifestations of what he saw as an emerging liberal spirit in Ireland, a spirit most of whose advocates, given the religious composition of Irish society at the time, were bound to be Catholic laypersons, supported of course by Protestants, from whom he expected little else, and by the odd heterodox Catholic cleric, from whom he expected much more.[4]

The fifth of ten children, Dinneen was born in the townland of Rath, four miles southwest of Rathmore in the Sliabh Luachra district of Co. Kerry on Christmas Day 1860. Educated in local schools, where his intellectual abilities were soon recognised, he showed an early interest in the priesthood, an interest doubtless encouraged by his deeply, indeed excessively, pious mother. While still at home in Carn he was tutored in Latin by a curate in Rathmore and came under the influence of the Jesuit Irish scholar Denis Murphy, who convinced him to join the Jesuit order. He did so in 1880 and was ordained in 1894, although his training continued until 1898. During this time he studied modern literature and mathematics – the former with Gerard Manley Hopkins – taking a degree with honours in 1885, followed by an MA in mathematics in 1889. At UCD he also taught as an assistant in mathematics before going on to serve on the faculty of Jesuit secondary schools, including Clongowes Wood, where he spent two years and where his interests shifted from maths to literature. Even more notable was his new interest in literature in Irish, an interest that seems to have been inspired by his fellow Clongowes teacher Father John McErlean, an accomplished Irish scholar who was then working on an edition of the poems of Geoffrey Keating.

In 1900 Dinneen left the Jesuit order, apparently amicably and with the consent of his superiors. His biographers Proinsias Ó Conluain and Donncha Ó Céileachair argue that this decision was based on his personal unsuitability for the regimented life of a religious order, quoting the Jesuit Father John J. Coyne as stating that Dinneen found the disciplined life of the order oppressive because he was 'solitary by nature' (aonaránach ó nádúr) and 'a bit eccentric as well' (beagáinín corr ann féin freisin), and that his superiors agreed and decided 'that better use could be made of his talents outside of a religious order' (gurbh fhearr an úsáid a d'fhéadfaí a bhaint as a chuid talanna taobh amuigh d'órd crábhaidh).[5] Dinneen nevertheless remained a priest and would have been allowed to administer the sacraments had he sought and received the permission of the bishop in whose diocese he resided. He apparently never did so though he always wore clerical garb and later somewhat disingenuously told those who requested his priestly intervention that he would 'hear' Mass for them! And Jesuit or not, he remained a vigorous and formidable defender of the rights and privileges of the Catholic Church in Ireland.

Whatever his superiors actually made of their prickly former colleague, they were certainly right about the proper field for his talents, as almost immediately after leaving the order he became a major – and highly controversial – figure within the language revival movement. Associating himself with the Gaelic League's Keating Branch, a group noted for both its Catholicism and its fervent support of the cause of Munster Irish, he became the branch president in 1904, a position he held until 1909. In addition he served on some of the League's most important committees, among them the Executive Committee (An Coiste Gnó) and the sub-committees for education, spelling reform, publication, and organisation. Like the Jesuits, his revivalist colleagues soon found he was, however gifted, a difficult and divisive presence. Indeed Piaras Béaslaí was to write of him that while he was on the Coiste Gnó he was usually in a 'magnificent minority of one'.[6] Particularly galling for his fellow language activists must have been his support for the Catholic hierarchy in their opposition to the Gaelic League's demand that Irish be made a required subject for matriculation in the new National University of Ireland. His decision here seems to have been motivated in part by his genuine loyalty to Church authorities and in part by his personal animosity towards Father Michael O'Hickey, whose dismissal from his teaching post at Maynooth became a focal point for those protesting the bishops' stand on essential Irish. At any rate, this controversy was to create a split within the ranks of the Keating Branch, leading to Dinneen's resignation as president and his withdrawal from active involvement in League affairs.[7]

Dinneen was to claim that from the time he left the Jesuits he made his living solely from writing in Irish. This would have been no mean accomplishment at the time, but Dinneen was a prolific writer on an impressive range of topics. His *magnum opus* was *Foclóir Gaedhilge – Béarla / Irish English Dictionary* (1927), the first and much shorter version of which appeared in 1904, when it was hailed by Patrick Pearse as 'an epoch of the movement'. The plates for this book were destroyed during the Easter Rising of 1916 so that Dinneen, with the help of Liam S. Gógan, had to compile the great dictionary of 1927 anew, his reward being that the work was to remain the standard dictionary of the language until the appearance of Niall Ó Dónaill's *Foclóir Gaeilge-Béarla* (*Irish-English Dictionary*) in 1977.[8] It remains in print and of value right to the present. Among Dinneen's other major publications were scholarly editions, some still canonical, of major writers like Aodhagán Ó Rathaile (1900, revised and enlarged edition 1911), Eoghan Ruadh Ó Súilleabháin (1901), Seán Clárach Mac Domhnaill (1902), Séafraidh Ó Donnchadha an Ghleanna (1902), Tadhg Gaelach Ó Súilleabháin (1903), Piaras Feirtéir (1903, revised and expanded version 1934), the Maigue poets (1906), and Geoffrey Keating (3 vols, 1908–14).[9] In addition he edited, with Irish and English translations, the Latin text of St Patrick's *Confessio* (1906, new edition 1934), and the eighteenth-century text *Me Guidhir Fhearmanach* (*The Maguires of Fermanagh*) (1917).

The most important of his creative works was doubtless his only novel, *Cormac Ó Conaill* (1901), not so much for any intrinsic literary value, but as the first novel ever written in Irish. He was also a pioneer of the Gaelic stage, publishing five plays in Irish: *Creideamh agus Gorta: Traigheadheacht a Bhaineas le hAimsir an Droch-Shaoghail*, 1847 (*Faith and Famine: A Tragedy Concerning the Time of the Famine*, 1847 (1901), *An Tobar Draoidheachta* (*The Magic Well*) (1902), *Girle Guairle* (*Hurly-Burly*) (1904), *Comhairle Fithil: Úrchluiche Dhá-Ghníomh* (*Fitheal's Counsel: An Original Play in Two Acts*) (1909), which was published in English translation the same year, and *Teachtaire ó Dhia: Dráma Bhaineas leis an nDroch-Shaoghal* (*A Messenger from God: A Play Concerning the Famine*) (nd). *Creideamh agus Gorta* was already in print when Douglas Hyde's *Casadh an tSúgáin* (*The Twisting of the Rope*) became the first play in Irish to be performed on a commercial stage in Dublin when it was produced in October 1901 by the Irish Literary Theatre. Dinneen's play was not, however, produced until 1903 and was never popular. More successful was the lighter *Tobar na Draoidheachta*, which had its premiere in Tralee in September 1902 and was performed by amateur groups from time to time thereafter. Both of these plays attracted the interest of Yeats, who in the issue *Samhain* for 1901 called *Creideamh agus Gorta* 'the best Gaelic play after Dr Hyde's' and who in the 1902 edition of the same journal wrote: 'Of the other plays in Irish acted during the year, Father Dinneen's *Tobar Draoidheachta* is probably the best . . . One admires its *naiveté* as much as anything else.' He also felt the play 'has more fancy and a more sustained energy than *Creideamh agus Gorta*'.[10]

Dinneen also published two books of entirely pedestrian poetry in Irish: *Startha as an Soiscéal i bhFilidheacht* (*Stories from the Gospel in Poetry*) (1917) and *Spioraid na Saoirse: Aisling Draiodheachta ar an mBliain 1916*) (*The Spirit of Freedom: A Magical Vision of 1916*) (1919), verse reflections on the Easter Rising. In addition, he produced a translation of Dickens's *A Christmas Carol* as *Duan na Nodlag* (1903), short books on Irish local, social, and cultural history, the

most important among them being the still useful *Cill Áirne*
(*Killarney*) (1902), *Saoghal i nÉirinn* (*Life in Ireland*), and *Muinntear
Chiarraidhe roimh an Droch-Shaoghal* (*The People of Kerry Before
the Famine*) (1905); language and history textbooks; propaganda
pamphlets like *Lectures on the Irish Language Movement* (1904), and
Native History in the National Schools (1905), a collection of original
essays on the classics, *Aisti ar Litridheacht Ghréigise is Laidne* (1929);
and most notable for our purposes here, more than a thousand columns that ran in D. P. Moran's weekly paper *The Leader* virtually
without interruption between 1906 and 1929. Moreover, he also left
behind several significant unpublished writings, the most interesting
of which is *The Queen of the Hearth* (National Library of Ireland MS
8623, folder 11).[11]

Dinneen remained an active scholar to the very end of his life in
1934, when he collapsed in the National Library while on his way to
the Reading Room and died shortly thereafter in St Vincent's
Hospital.[12] Despite his many eccentricities, not least of which was a
miserliness that prompted him to expect others to provide him with
everything from clothing to food to tram tickets,[13] he remained a
popular and highly respected figure in Irish intellectual life, awarded
an honorary D.Litt by the National University in 1919 and given a
lavish funeral at the Jesuit Church on Gardiner Street[14] attended
by Éamon de Valera, then President of the Executive Council of
Saorstát Éireann, and Seán T. O'Kelly, the future president of the
country, as well as by many scholars, priests, language revivalists,
and ordinary citizens.[15]

Returning to *The Queen of the Hearth*, we see that internal
evidence makes it obvious that the work was written during World
War I, though it is difficult to say precisely when. Dinneen was
careful to eliminate local topical references in this essay, writing not
from an Irish but from a British, European, or even pan-Western
perspective – and in English – on what he clearly saw as an issue of

pressing importance in modern industrial and industrialising societies. Still it is hard to see how he could have entirely ignored an Irish event of the magnitude of the 1916 Easter Rising, an event that was to have an enormous influence on his thinking about politics and nationalism.[16] It may well be, then, that the essay was written before or early in 1916, although we simply cannot be certain it was not done anytime between 1915 and November 1918, by which time he had come to terms with the fact of female suffrage. The question that next occurs is why Dinneen never published the piece. Despite its length it could easily have been serialised in a contemporary periodical or published, as were other of his works, as a pamphlet. Perhaps the easiest answer to this question is that not having put the piece in print during the war, he realised that the vastly changed and still rapidly changing world of post-war Europe had rendered it largely irrelevant as a detailed statement of a position unlikely to attract much attention.[17] It does, however, deserve a new look now – not because it ever could or should make any converts, but because it is the most developed and detailed exposition by an Irish-Irelander of what was at one time an important if not dominant school of thought on women's role in modern society, a school of thought that was to have a major influence on the thinking of that other remarkable Irish-Ireland individual Éamon de Valera when he came to formulate the sections on women and the family in *Bunreacht na hÉireann* in 1937.[18]

Curiously, Dinneen's columns in *The Leader* offer us less insight than might be expected into his thinking on issues involving women. A true pioneer as the first real current affairs columnist in Irish, he used his weekly contributions to engage with an impressive range of topics of interest to himself and the Irish public. Thus over the years he wrote regularly and pointedly on contemporary events, primarily in Ireland, but also in Britain, the United States, and further afield. For example, he offered his opinions on Home Rule, labour issues, social problems like poverty and education, and the Irish War of Independence and Civil War, as well as on British and American politics and racial discrimination in the United States. But he also wrote on moral questions, anthropology, Irish, English, and Classical literature, and the usual occasional topics that draw the attention of any good journalist. However, given the keen interest so obvious in *The Queen of the Hearth*, he said surprisingly little about suffrage and the larger issue of women's place in society in *The Leader*, devoting only a few essays in whole or in part to these questions.

Such restraint with regard to this contemporary 'hot-button' issue is particularly striking in comparison with the rhetorical excesses to which it drove *The Leader*'s editor D. P. Moran, a close friend of Dinneen and in some ways his political mentor.[19] For Moran, suffragists, whether British or Irish, were the 'shrieking sisterhood' (*Leader*, 13/4/12), a 'gang of obnoxious females' (*Leader*, 6/7/12), 'the virago Suffers' (*Leader*, 3/8/12), and 'freaks, cranks, and a few of the Ascendancy' (*Leader*, 1/2/13). The editor and others who wrote regularly for *The Leader* were particularly savage in their attacks on the male feminist Francis Sheehy-Skeffington (always 'Skeffy' to them), who was pilloried in articles, verses, and cartoons, as effeminate, freakish, and absurd. For Moran, he was 'the ubiquitous Skeffy . . . a sort of spook in whiskers and knickerbockers' (*Leader*, 9/12/11), about whom he could write: 'It would be difficult, if not impossible, to avoid being somewhat personal in reference to Skeffy – he seems to invite it with his aggressive whiskers, his high-pitched querulous voice, and his, we had almost said, his immortal, knickerbockers' (*Leader*, 20/2/09). Every bit as dismissive was 'A. M. W.,' who contributed doggerel and skits to the paper attacking the suffragists in general and Sheehy-Skeffington in particular in verses like the following:

No doubt since the Suffers appeared in the field,
Most wonderful phases has Skeffy revealed.
How oft have we seen in some outlandish prank
The strange evolution of Skeffy the crank (*Leader*, 5/7/13).[20]

Moran's opposition to the militant Irish suffragists was rooted in a blend of principle, pragmatism, and prejudice. In the first place, he was convinced that they were enemies of his Irish-Ireland philosophy since they were, in his mind, little more than a wholly controlled subsidiary of the British movement. Thus in January 1911, he wrote:

> The Suffragettes in Ireland, though scarcely of Ireland, are too utterly obviously a mere imitation of the English brand. If the English ladies had not led the way . . . the Suffragettes of Dublin would not be dogging the steps of poor Mr Sheehy, MP, and others of the Irish Party . . . Who are the Irish Suffragettes? . . . We fear they are mostly self-advertisers trying to imitate their English sisters (*Leader*, 28/1/11).[21]

When the following year in Dublin the English suffragist Mary Leigh threw a hatchet into the coach carrying Prime Minister Herbert Asquith and the Irish Party leader John Redmond, slightly injuring the latter, and later she and her colleague from the Women's Social and Political Union attempted to set fire to the curtains at the Theatre Royal, where Asquith was to deliver a speech about Home Rule, Moran was quick to point out that neither woman was Irish, continuing:

> With the Suffragette movement in England we have little concern, but when two Englishwomen come over to Ireland to carry on their quarrel in a most criminal manner with the English Prime Minister, who

happens to be in Ireland on a Home Rule Mission, we think they richly deserve the sentences that have been passed upon them (*Leader*, 17/8/12).[22]

What he failed to mention here is that the Irish Women's Franchise League explicitly disavowed any involvement in these actions.[23]

These references to Home Rule and the Irish Party show Moran's very practical political concern that Irish feminists could damage the Home Rule campaign through their attacks on the Party, and particularly on its leader John Redmond, an intransigent opponent of women's suffrage in the British Parliament.[24] For example, when in 1913 Irish suffragists actively opposed the Liberal Party candidate supported by Redmond in a by-election in Derry, Moran was outraged:

> The excursion of Suffers into Derry is but one more piece of evidence of the political fatuity of these people. They saw a great chance – as they thought – to be important. In such a close fight as Derry was bound to be every individual vote was important . . . It gave opportunity to the 'non-political and non-sectarian' Suffers in this country, and they did their little trick of proclaiming war on the Home Rule candidate (*Leader*, 8/2/13).[25]

Moran himself was actually no great admirer of Redmond, but he believed that for strategic reasons all Irish people should unite behind him and his party in the cause of Home Rule, postponing until after the establishment of an Irish parliament any agitation for what he saw as secondary goals. Consequently he regularly affirmed that 'when we get Home Rule will be the time to consider the question of votes for women in Ireland' (*Leader*, 10/2/12).[26] Indeed he could go even farther, writing the following year: 'In Ireland under Home Rule we do not believe there would be much difficulty in the matter, even in face of the antics of the notoriety hunters and foreigners who have made a farce of the votes for women movement in the country' (*Leader*, 26/4/13). In the meantime, he saw such antics as all but treasonous and believed that suffragists should be patient, keep quiet, and back their archenemy Redmond, however unlikely it was that he would ever support women's suffrage in a Home Rule parliament.[27]

When not provoked by a new case of feminist activism, Moran could try to convince himself that Irish suffragists were merely a rather minor irritant, writing in 1914, for example, that 'the Suffers don't count in Ireland except as a slight nuisance now and again' (*Leader*, 6/6/14). Indeed he regularly repeated the idea that

> the screeching sisterhood do not appear to have taken much root in Ireland . . . So far as we can judge Irish women – real Irish women – are not to any extent anxious to mix up in active politics, and look with amused contempt on most of those few women in Ireland who, in sympathy with the English screeching sisterhood . . . have taken up the matter here (*Leader*, 2/10/12).

Beneath notice are his attempts and those of his colleagues at *The Leader*, particularly the cartoonists, to dismiss all suffragists as 'unsexed' and physically unattractive to men.[28]

Father Dinneen shared many of Moran's ideas – no surprise given their close professional and personal relationship. As a Home Ruler, he was worried that suffrage activism – most notably the hatchet attack on Asquith and Redmond and the attempt to burn the Theatre Royal – could hurt the cause.[29] Like many others, he was also concerned that the redistribution of parliamentary seats that would be necessitated by the granting of female suffrage might diminish Irish representation in the Imperial Parliament.[30] On the whole, however, whereas Moran's opposition to suffragism was primarily pragmatic and focused narrowly on the Irish women's movement, Dinneen's was more broadly philosophical, and as a result he raised issues that extended well beyond the right of women to vote in Irish elections.

Of course Dinneen's distaste for feminism was not entirely intellectual.[31] Much of it was no doubt prompted by his identification of the women's movement with other contemporary causes that troubled him. And there was no shortage of those. Moreover, such linkages were by no means figments of his imagination.[32] For example, Irish feminists like Louie Bennett and Hannah Sheehy-Skeffington were deeply involved in labour and trades union issues. The activist Irish Women's Franchise League (founded 1908) and its journal *The Irish Citizen* (founded 1912) consistently supported the labour movement in general and especially the Irish Women Workers' Union (founded 1911), with which it shared many members.[33] Dinneen's attitude to the labour movement was complex and sometimes contradictory. As an orthodox Catholic clergyman he utterly rejected anything smacking of socialism. Thus in May 1911, he wrote:

> Too much work is being put on the State of late; already the support of the old people has been put on it . . . By degrees a load of expense will be put on the State as well as more responsibility. It is a bad thing to put too much work of that kind on the State, for that extra work will divert it from its own proper work. . .

> (Tá an iomad oibre dá cur ar an Stát le déidheannaighe; tá cothughadh na sean-daoine curtha cheana féin air . . . Beifear ag cur ualaigh costais ar an Stát i ndiaidh a chéile, agus ag cur cúraim san mbreis air chomh maith. Is olc an rud an iomad oibre den tsaghas soin do chur ar an Stát; mar cuirfidh an bhreis oibre sin ó n-a obair chirt féin é. . .) (*Leader*, 20/5/11).[34]

Yet he also had a genuine compassion for the poor and oppressed and could be sharply critical of the conditions in which they lived and worked. For example, he devoted a column in 1911 to the Triangle Shirtwaist Factory fire in New York, deploring the plight of the female workers who lost their lives trapped in that sweatshop (*Leader*, 15/4/11).[35] More typical of his thinking, however, were his rather maudlin accounts of urban poverty,[36] a condition for which he sometimes suggested some kind of state intervention, but generally felt should be the province of voluntary Christian charity from the better off.[37] That a significant number of Irish feminists were well to the left of him could only have increased his suspicion of them.

He would also have disliked the strong and vocal pacifist convictions of many Irish suffragists, convictions given forceful expression in *The Irish Citizen*, one of whose editors, Francis Sheehy-Skeffington, wrote just after the outbreak of war in 1914: 'War is necessarily bound up with the destruction of feminism . . . Feminism is necessarily bound up with the abolition of war' (*IC*, 12/9/14). In 1915 activists like Louie Bennett founded the Irish branch of the Women's International League for Peace and Freedom. Unlike Sheehy-Skeffington and women like Bennett and others from the pacifist Irish Women's Franchise League,[38] Dinneen was in the mainstream of British and European thinking about militarism and war on the eve of and during World War I. In 1911 he could write dispassionately in response to the pacifist views of Andrew Carnegie: 'As you say, war is a wicked thing, and it is best to avoid it if possible. But is it possible to avoid war? Doubtless it is now and again, but it is nonsense to say that it is always possible to avoid war' (Fé mar adeirir is olc an rud cogadh, agus is fearr é sheachaint má's féidir é. Acht an féidir cogadh do sheachaint? Is féidir anois is arís gan amhras, acht is díth chéille a rádh gur féidir cogadh a sheachaint i gcomhnuidhe) (*Leader*, 25/3/11). But by the following year he had already become more bellicose, capable of seeing war in conventional terms as a test of manhood and source of glory:

It is a fine thing to die on the field of battle for our country or our faith. The memory of the person who dies that kind of death will never be eclipsed and his story and his fame will be told in the assemblies and in the gatherings of the citizens to give courage to the young and inspire them to great deeds and valour.

(Is breágh an rud é bás d'fhagháil ar mhachaire an chomhraic ar son ár dtíre nó ár gcreidimh. An té gheibheann a leithéid sin de bhás ní rachaidh a chuimhne i mbáthadh go bráth agus beidh a stair is a thuairisc dá n-aithris i mórdhálaibh is i gcruinnighthe na saorfhear chum meisneach do chur ar an aos óg, is iad do ghríosughadh chum deighghníomhartha is chum gaisce) (*Leader*, 16/11/12).

He did, however, change his tune as he learned of the butchery on the Western Front, and while never espousing pacifism, in effect he devoted most of his columns on the war to its carnage and cost.[39] Nevertheless, he could still see the Great War as part of God's plan:

The God of glory is looking down angrily on the fields of battle and on the destructive work going on there, and without a doubt that scourge has been well deserved by the states now fighting each other . . . and with God's help every state will be better for the terror they are experiencing.

(Tá Dia na glóire ag féachaint anuas go feargach ar mhachairibh an chomhraic agus ar an obair mhilltigh atá ar siubhal ionnta agus gan aon amhras is maith atá an sgiúirse sin tuillte ag na státaibh atá i n-achrann i n-a chéile fá láthair . . . agus le congnamh Dé tiocfaidh feabhas ar gach aon stát de bharr an scannartha atá dá fhagháil aca) (*Leader*, 14/11/14).

 We find a similar ambivalence about war at the beginning of *The Queen of the Hearth*, where he sees the production of soldiers as one of the greatest contributions mothers make to the state.

Predictably enough, many of the Irish suffragists were, like Mary Hayden, Eibhlín Nic Niocaill, and Agnes O'Farrelly, at the forefront of efforts to increase educational opportunities for Irish women, particularly at the university level.[40] Here again their activities would have aroused the concern of Fr Dinneen. The place of women in the educational system is a central concern in *The Queen of the Hearth*, but Dinneen also dealt with the question from time to time in his columns, as when he wrote of co-education in 1910 in terms similar to those he was to use in *The Queen of the Hearth*:

> But I think that harm would come from co-education for girls and for boys in every kind of learning in every way during their youth and adolescence, and that it would do little good. It would not benefit the girls. It would set them to learning subjects that would not suit them and that would not be good for their health and that would break their hearts before they reached a woman's age.

> (Acht comhoideachas i ngach cineál léighinn ins gach aon tslighe le linn a n-óige is le linn a n-ógántachta do chailínibh is do bhuachaillibh, is dóigh liom go dtiocfadh díoghbháil as agus nach mór an maitheas a dhéanfadh sé. Ní ar ród a leasa do sheolfadh sé na cailínidhe. Chuirfeadh sé ag foghluim cineál léighinn iad ná hoirfeadh dóibh is ná raghadh chum maitheasa dá sláinte is do bhrisfeadh an croidhe ionnta sar a mbeadh aois mná sroiste aca) (*Leader*, 18/6/10).[41]

The years immediately before Dinneen wrote *The Queen of the Hearth* were turbulent ones for the suffrage and broader feminist movements in both Britain and Ireland, with large marches, acts of civil disobedience and public vandalism, prison protests, and even deaths. Needless to say Dinneen must have followed these developments closely and usually with dismay. For example, in 1910 he took note of a Dublin lecture by Cristabel Pankhurst, praising her oratorical skills while claiming rather disingenuously that he wouldn't say anything about her message because 'we don't have time' (níl sé d'uainn againn) (*Leader*, 19/3/10). Needless to say, he disapproved of the window-smashing occasionally engaged in by suffragists in both Ireland and Britain, although it is worth noting that he felt the six-month sentences handed down to some of those convicted for this crime were much too harsh (*Leader*, 27/7/12).[42] Nor is it any surprise that he was appalled by the attack on Asquith and Redmond and the arson attempt on the Theatre Royal and thankful the perpe-trators were not Irish (*Leader*, 27/7/12). The following year he commented briefly on the death of Emily Davison, trampled while trying to throw a suffrage banner over the king's horse in the Epsom Derby (*Leader*, 28/6/13), and also used his column to make light of the way imprisoned suffragists used the hunger strike to secure their freedom, writing: 'Here's to hunger; fasting is the best of tricks! It is stronger than locks and iron doors . . . The weakest woman at the fair is stronger with strength from fasting than the army of the king of England' (Mo ghreidhin an t-ocras; rogha na gcleas an troscadh! Is treise é 'ná glais is 'ná dóirse iarainn . . . An bhean is laige ar an aonach is treise í le neart ón dtroscadh 'ná arm rí Shasana) (*Leader*, 10/5/13).[43]

When, however, he came to write *The Queen of the Hearth*, he virtually ignored the often spectacular specifics of suffrage agitation to focus on broader philosophical, moral, and social questions. So committed was he to this more universal approach that he eliminated everything that might identify him not only as an Irish-language activist, but even as Irish at all, writing instead, as was noted above, very much from a British or even broadly Western perspective.[44] Less successful was his attempt to disguise his class bias. Indeed he may have been so blind to his bias on this question that he felt no need for concealment. Again and again in *The Queen of the Hearth* he makes clear where his class allegiance lies. He might be willing to admit that some poor women had to work outside the home, and he does acknowledge that 'domestic happiness may be found in the humblest no less than in the most exalted homes', but as he states in the chapter on 'The Fundamental School': 'The dignity and responsibility of motherhood in the family should belong to one who is free from external cares and wholly devoted to her domestic duties.' In his mind – despite his own humble rural childhood – the ideal 'home' seems always to have been that of a comfortable middle-class family. To borrow a phrase from his own rigorous brand of Catholicism, there might be survival outside of bourgeois domesticity, but there could be never be salvation.

At any rate, in *The Queen of the Hearth*, his concern is not with transient current events, but with the whole question of what would be the place of women in a world he knew could never be the same in the aftermath of the Great War. Accordingly his chapters deal with women's role in the family, in the school, in the workplace, and indeed in society as a whole, where they would live as daughters, wives, single women, workers, and widows, but above all as mothers. Unfortunately, however, despite his ambitious aims in this essay, he had virtually nothing new to say, remaining throughout merely yet another spokesman for a philosophy then still widespread if not prevalent, but soon to be rendered ever more anachronistic, a philosophy that saw men and women in starkly dichotomous terms, living their lives in separate (though by no means equal) spheres.[45] The suffragists' great bugbear Herbert Asquith gave succinct expression to this theory and its political consequences in 1892:

> The inequalities which democracy requires that we should fight against and remove are the unearned privileges and the artificial distinctions which man has made, and which man can unmake. They are not those indelible differences of faculty and function by which Nature herself has given diversity and richness to human society.[46]

Or, as Dinneen put it in his chapter on 'Woman and the Hearth', 'no matter what legislation may devise, domestic life is the highest ideal of their [women's] happiness . . . The hearth is their sphere of life, the theatre of their joys and triumphs. Nature has planted in their souls an instinct which never gets its full satisfaction outside the sacred precincts of home life.'[47] In his plays and fiction, Dinneen created several strong female characters, most notably the mother in *Creideamh agus Gorta* who during the Famine chooses death by starvation for herself and her children over the nourishment offered her by Soupers, and the wife in *Teachtaire ó Dhia* who in a time of famine practises charity against the wishes of her husband, only to be rewarded when it turns out the woman she fed is St Brigid. But these women never really move beyond their separate and domestic sphere, performing their ordained functions as either protector (of the faith if not the lives) of their families, or as nurturers. In 1912 the feminist paper *The Irish Citizen* published an editorial entitled 'Discovery of the Femaculine', proclaiming:

> The Femaculine. The synthesis of the virtues of the masculine and the feminine, in which the defects of each are balanced if not eliminated. Hurt one, and you hurt both, for they 'are members one of another'. Do good to one, and you do good to all. On this bed-rock of scientific truth rest the movements for the social amelioration of modern conditions and for the freeing of womanhood (*IC*, 12/6/12).[48]

While we do not know whether Dinneen ever read this paper or heard of this concept, we can be sure about what he would have thought of both, for it is precisely in vigorous refutation of this 'bed-rock of scientific truth' that he took up his pen to write *The Queen of the Hearth*.

Notes to Introduction

1 W. P. Ryan, *The Pope's Green Island* (Boston, n. d.) p. 122.

2 Ibid., p. 125.

3 Ibid. See also Proinsias Ó Conluain and Donncha Ó Céileachair, *An Duinníneach: An tAthair Pádraig Ó Duinnín, a Shaol, a Shaothar agus an Ré inar Mhair Sé* (*Dinneen: Father Patrick Dinneen, His Life, his Work and the Period in which he Lived*) (Baile Átha Cliath, 1958), pp 165–9.

4 Some Irish Catholic priests did indeed support the call for women's suffrage. See Cliona Murphy, *The Women's Suffrage Movement and Irish Society in the Early Twentieth Century* (Philadelphia, 1989), p. 153. See also J. Eliot Ross, CSP, 'An American priest on votes for women', *The Irish Citizen* (hereafter *IC*), 19, 26 Dec. 1914; 2 Jan. and 9 Jan. 1915; and 'A New Zealand priest', 'Votes for women in practice', *IC*, 1 May 1915.

5 Ó Conluain and Ó Céileachair, *An Duinníneach*, pp 124–9.

6 Piaras Béaslaí, quoted by Eoin Mac Cárthaigh, in James McGuire and James Quinn (eds.), *Dictionary of Irish Biography*, vol. 3 (Cambridge, 2009), p. 329.

7 See the entry for Pádraig Ó Duinnín in Diarmuid Breathnach and Máire Ní Mhurchú, *Beathaisnéis a Trí* (*Biography 3*) (Baile Átha Cliath, 1992), pp 97–8. O'Hickey had been sharply critical of Dinneen's 1904 Irish-English dictionary in his review of the book for the *Irish Ecclesiastical Record*. See Mícheál Briody, 'The lexicographical contention of Mícheál Ó hIceadha and Pádraig Ó Duinnín', in *Dinneen and the Dictionary 1904–2004* (ed.) Pádraigín Riggs, *Irish Texts Society Subsidary* Series 16 (2005), pp 14–50.

8 See Noel O'Connell, *Father Dinneen: His Dictionary and the Gaelic Revival* (London, n.d.), Riggs (ed.), *Dinneen and the Dictionary 1904–2004*, and Liam Mac Amhlaigh, *Foclóirí agus Foclóirithe na Gaeilge* (*Irish-Language Dictionaries and Lexicographers*) (Baile Átha Cliath, 2008), pp 93–103. The dictionary was in its quirkiness very much the creation of its compiler, whom Brian Ó Nualláin ('Myles na gCopaleen') famously called 'our great comic lexicographer', using his column in *The Irish Times* to draw attention to offbeat entries from the dictionary to support his case. Alf Mac Lochlainn provides a glimpse at some of the fascinating information about Gaelic life and culture that Dinneen sheds passing light on in his dictionary in *Farasbarr Feasa ar Éirinn: Sleachta as Leabhar Rúnda ina bhFuil Léiriú ar Mheon Lucht Labhartha na Gaeilge Anallód go hÁirithe a nGráin do na Mnáibh agus a nGean do na Prátaí* (*A Surplus of Knowledge about Ireland: Extracts from a Secret Book in which there is an Illustration of the Mind of Irish-Speakers, in Particular their Hatred of Women and their Fondness for Potatoes*) (Dublin, 2005).

9   He edited the second, third, and fourth volumes of Keating's *Foras Feasa ar Éirinn / The History of Ireland* for the Irish Texts Society, taking over from David Comyn, who had edited the first volume (1901).

10 See Yeats, *The Collected Works of W. B. Yeats*, vol. 8: *The Irish Dramatic Movement*, (eds) Mary Fitzgerald and Richard J. Finneran (New York, 2003), pp 7, 15.

11 For our purposes here the most important of the other unpublished writings are the fragments of an anti-suffrage play in English, published here as an appendix, and his essays in English on temperance and in Irish on his mother, both of which will be referred to and quoted from below.

12 That Dinneen was a well-known and on occasion rather demanding presence in the National Library is evident from the following brief passage from the Scylla and Charybdis episode of Joyce's *Ulysses*: 'Mr Lyster! Father Dinneen wants . . .' 'O! Father Dinneen! Directly.' Joyce owned a copy of Dinneen's *A Smaller Irish-English Dictionary for the Use of Schools* (1910). Alf Mac Lochlainn recalls being told by library assistant Pádraig Ó Conchubhair that one of the duties of boy attendants at the library was to follow Dinneen when he left the reading room and pick up the slips of paper he dropped on which he had written notes and entries for his dictionary. See Mac Lochlainn, 'Father Dinneen and his dictionary', *Studies: An Irish Quarterly Review*, 91: 361 (Spring, 2002), p. 68.

13 He once even entered a literary competition for children, which he won and whose token cash prize he pocketed.

14 The Jesuits treated him as one of their own at the end of his life, offering spiritual comfort in his final days and purchasing his grave for him in Glasnevin Cemetery.

15 The information for this biographical sketch has been drawn from Ó Conluain and Ó Céileachair, *An Duinníneach*, Breathnach and Ní Mhurchú, *Beathaisnéis a Trí* , pp 96–8, Eoin Mac Cárthaigh's entry on Dinneen in *Dictionary of Irish Biography*, vol. 3, pp 328–30; and Henry Boylan, *A Dictionary of Irish Biography*, 3rd edn (Dublin, 1998), pp 111–2.

16 As noted above, he published a tribute in verse to the Rising as *Spiorad na Saoirse: Aisling Draoidheachta ar an mBliain 1916* in 1919. See also his columns in *The Leader* for 20 May, 27 May, 29 July, 5 Aug., 23 Sept. and 16 Dec. 1916.

17 In a 1919 column entitled 'Togha mór na mban' ('The great women's election'), Dinneen wrote of the recent general election of 1918, the first in which women over 30 could vote, opining that women would not have won the vote if not for the war, but accepting female suffrage as a *fait accompli*. Indeed

he went farther, arguing that women should also be allowed to sit in parliament and that making them wait until the age of 30 to exercise a right granted to men at 21 was an 'insult' (*masla*) to them (*Leader*, 11 Jan. 1919). On the other hand, given the restrictions placed on women's rights under the Cumann na nGaedheal Government of Saorstát Éireann in the 1920s, a government he supported, he may well have thought the publication was unnecessary, since many of his ideas had been given force of law. See Maryann Gialanella Valiulis, '"Virtuous mothers and dutiful wives": The politics of sexuality in the Irish Free State', in *Gender and Power in Irish History*, (ed.) Valiulis (Dublin, 2009), pp 100–14.

18 The dubious distinction of being the Irish person who wrote the most widely known anti-suffrage tract belongs to Sir Almoth Wright, whose 1912 pamphlet *An Unexpurgated Case Against Women's Suffrage* drew fire from his fellow Dublin native George Bernard Shaw. See Cliona Murphy, *The Women's Suffrage Movement and Irish Society in the Early Twentieth century* (Philadelphia, 1989), pp 115–6. For more on Wright, see Hector Hughes, 'Sir Almoth Wright and woman suffrage', a paper read to a meeting of the Irish Women's Franchise League (Hereafter IWFL) in 1913 and published in *IC*, 24 Jan. and 14 Feb. 1914; David Morgan, *Suffragists and Liberals: The Politics of Woman Suffrage in England* (Oxford, 1975), pp 97–8; and Brian Harrison, *Separate Spheres: The Opposition to Women's Suffrage in Britain* (London, 1978), p. 67.

19 See Ó Conluain and Ó Céileachair, *An Duinníneach*, pp 170–5, 240.

20 Writing of a suffrage meeting in Belfast, Moran stated of Padraic Colum, 'the minor poet:' 'Perhaps it is only in the fitness of things that nearly all the men who are prominent Suffragettes, so far as we know, strike us as persons who really ought to dress in petticoats' (*Leader*, 24 Feb. 1912). For British anti-suffrage views of suffragists as the 'bustling clique of masculine women and feminine men,' see Brian Harrison, *Separate Spheres: The Opposition to Women's Suffrage in Britain* (London, 1978), pp 56–7.

21 He was, of course, wrong here. Cliona Murphy has shown that the Irish suffrage movement was proportionately as large as the one in England, of which it was independent. Murphy writes: 'Proximity and a common government necessitated a certain amount of interaction between the Irish and British suffragists, but it did not make them members of a single movement' (p. 7.) Others did, however, share the belief that Irish suffragists were leading their followers 'Englandwards.' See Cliona Murphy, '"The tune of the stars and stripes": The American influence on the Irish suffrage movement', in *Women Surviving: Studies in Irish Women's History in the 19th and 20th Centuries*, Maria

[21 *cont.*] Luddy and Cliona Murphy (eds) (Swords, 1989), p. 182. In 1912 *IC* felt compelled to spell out the facts: 'The suffrage movement in Ireland is one of native growth, managed and controlled within Ireland, and wholly indepen-dent of inspiration from outside' (*IC*, 14 Sept., 1912).

22 The women went on hunger strike after their convictions and were force fed. See Rosemary Cullen Owens, *Smashing Times: A History of the Irish Women's Suffrage Movement 1889–1922* (Dublin, 1984), pp 62–4. They were, however, to be the only suffragists force fed in Irish, as opposed to British jails. See Murphy, *The Women's Suffrage Movement*, pp 14–6. It is worth noting that according to David Morgan, as early as 1909 'the Home Secretary was clearly concerned at the possibility of real personal danger to the Prime Minister from suffragists' (p. 59.) For confrontations between British suffragists and politicians, see David Morgan, *Suffragists and Liberals: The Politics of Woman Suffrage in England* (Oxford, 1975), pp 71–2, 104–5. See also Harrison, *Separate Spheres*, p. 217.

23 See Dana Hearne, *The Development of Irish Feminist Thought: A Critical Analysis of The Irish Citizen, 1912–1920* (Ann Arbor, 1998), p. 27. *IC* took pains to stress that the attackers were English (*IC*, 27 July 1912), but also made light of the incident, claiming that the weapon used was 'a toy-hatchet, such as is used for breaking toffee' (*IC*, 10 Aug. 1912). For *IC*, the real story of that day was the violence inflicted on the suffragists by angry mobs.

24 According to Cliona Murphy, most members of the IWFL were in favour of Home Rule even if they rejected the Irish Party's leadership in this campaign. See Murphy, *The Women's Suffrage Movement*, p. 34. For relations between the suffrage movement and Redmond and his party, see Owens, *Smashing Times*, pp 48–50; Margaret Ward, 'Hannah Sheehy-Skeffington', in *Female Activists: Irish Women and Change 1900–1960*, Mary Cullen and Maria Luddy (eds) (Dublin, 2001), pp 92–3; Murphy, *The Women's Suffrage Movement*, pp 7–8, 149–50, 164, 172–3, 177–8, 187–9; Dana Hearne, *The Development of Irish Feminist Thought: A Critical Analysis of The Irish Citizen, 1912–1920* (Ann Arbor, 1998), pp 25–6; Sandra Stanley Holton, *Feminism and Democracy: Women's Suffrage and Reform Politics in Britain 1900–1918* (Cambridge, 1986), p. 72, Morgan, *Suffragists and Liberals*, pp 30–1, 97–9, 105–6, 112–3, 147, 152–3; and Harrison, *Separate Spheres*, p. 44.

25 See also his comments in *The Leader*, 10 Feb., 13 Apr., and 20 Apr. 1912. For the suffragists' perspective on their activity in Derry, see 'The siege of Derry,' *IC*, 1 Feb. 1913.

26 See also his comments in *The Leader*, 9 Mar., 20 Apr. and 18 May 1912; 1 Feb. and 26 Apr. 1913. Eibhlín Nic Niocaill dealt with this idea with some

ambivalence in a piece entitled 'An bhan-Ghaodhal' ('The female Gael') in the Feb. 1909 issue of *Bean na hÉireann*. For Nic Niocaill, see Micheál Ó Dubhshláine, *Óigbhean Uasal ó Phríomhchathair Éireann: Bás Eibhlín Nic Niocaill agus Dhomhnaill Chriomhthain ar an mBlascaod, 13 Lúnasa, 1909*) (*A Noble Young Woman from the Capital City of Ireland: The Drowning of Eibhlín Nic Niocaill and Domhnall Criomhthain on the Great Blasket, 9 August, 1909*) (Baile Átha Cliath, 1992).

27 For a graphic idea of how Irish suffragists viewed Redmond, see 'Our special St Patrick's Day cartoon/The angel of freedom', in which a winged Redmond stands with his foot on the bound body of a suffragist, holding in his hand a banner that reads in capital letters 'Hurro! For Liberty!!! No Irish Women Need Apply. No Votes for Women by Order of the New Liberator' (*IC*, 15 Mar. 1913). Two months later, an *IC* editorial proclaimed that 'nearly all suffragists must now agree . . . that Mr Redmond is the enemy of Woman Suffrage, and that, for constitutional as well as militant societies, the only honourable and logical course is opposition to the Redmond-Asquith coalition' (*IC*, 5 Oct. 1913). *IC* editorials and articles critical of Redmond and his party are far too numerous to list.

28 See also the cartoons in *The Leader*, 8 Feb., 17 May, 26 July, and 13 Dec. 1913; 14 Mar. and 12 Dec. 1914. This kind of abuse was a common tactic of those opposed to women's suffrage. See Harrison, *Separate Spheres*, pp 138–9, 195.

29 For Dinneen's support for Redmond and Home Rule, see Ó Conluain and Ó Céileachair, *An Duinníneach*, p. 232. That support was often qualified. See his columns in *The Leader* for 8 Aug. 1908; 20 Apr. and 28 Dec. 1912; 30 May and 1 Aug. 1914; 2 Jan. and 25 Sept. 1915; 10 June, 24 July, 30 June, 5 Aug. and 14 Oct. 1916. He was always suspicious of Asquith's intentions regarding Home Rule for Ireland. See his columns for 26 Feb. and 5 Mar. 1910; 16 Dec. 1916; and 6 July 1918. For his response to the attack and attempted arson, see his column in *The Leader*, 27 July 1912.

30 See his comments in 'Guth ag gach duine fásta' ('A vote for every adult'), *Leader*, 2/12/11.

31 He had no objection to females themselves and had a good number of women as friends, virtually all of them respectable spinsters properly deferential to him as priest and scholar. See Ó Conluain and Ó Céileachair, *An Duinníneach*, pp 20–1, 255–6, 266. Biddy Jenkinson has great fun with Dinneen and his lady friends in her story collection *An tAthair Pádraig Ó Duinnín, Bleachtaire* (*Father Patrick Dinneen, Detective*) (Baile Átha Cliath, 2008).

32 I will not be discussing what at the time were more fringe causes championed by some suffragists, causes like vegetarianism, spiritualism,

[32 *cont.*] agnosticism, eugenics, sex education, sexual abstinence in marriage, birth control, divorce, and lesbianism, all of which would have would have annoyed, angered, and/or appalled Dinneen. See Murphy, *The Women's Suffrage Movement*, p. 28, p. 140; and Harrison, *Separate Spheres*, p. 36. On the other hand, he, like Moran, would have agreed with feminist support for temperance. See his unpublished essay headed 'Abstinence' in the National University of Ireland (MS 8623, folder 9), where he writes of 'a house in which one or more drunkards reside' that 'a curse has lighted on that house whose fruits are gloom on every face, the sinister light of suspicion in every eye, sadness in every heart'. Since we know that Dinneen himself enjoyed an occasional drink, it is no surprise to read here that while he believed the Catholic clergy should take the lead in any temperance movement, 'of course I do not mean that all the clergy would be expected to become total abstainers on the spot. I mean nothing so unreasonable.' Temperance was one of his favourite themes in his columns. For a few examples, see *Leader*, 4 July 1914; 13 Apr. 1915; 9 June 1917; 1 Feb. 1919; 17 Jan. 1920; 4 Mar. 1922; 7 July, 14 July, 21 July, 28 July, 4 Aug., 11 Aug., 18 Aug., 25 Aug., 1 Sept., 8 Sept., and 22 Sept. 1923; 2 Feb. 24, and 31 Mar. 1928. See also Ó Conluain and Ó Céileachair, *An Duinníneach*, pp 242–5. Some Catholic and Protestant clergymen were apparently attracted to the suffrage movement by its support for temperance. See Murphy, *The Women's Suffrage Movement*, p. 157. See also Louie Bennett, 'Woman suffrage and the drink question', *IC*, 22 Aug. 1914.

33 The IWFL also at one point shared office space with the Irish Socialist Party. See R. M. Fox, *Rebel Irishwomen* (Dublin, 1967 [1935]), p. 75. For connections between the suffrage and labour movements, see Alison Buckley, '"Let the girls come forth:" The early feminist ideology of the Irish Women's Workers' Union', *in Irish Women's History*, Alan Hayes and Diane Urquhart (eds), (Dublin, 2004), pp 103–14; Owens, *Smashing Times*, pp 74–94; and Murphy, *The Women's Suffrage Movement*, pp 118–22. Dana Hearne defines the paper's editorial stance as 'feminist, pacifist, and socialist' (Hearne, *The Development of Irish Feminist Thought*, p. 123, n. 3). It should also be noted here that according to Hearne the circulation of *IC* in June 1913 was around 3,000, equal to that of the far better known *Sinn Féin* (Hearne, p. 37).

34 See also his *Leader* column 9 Feb. 1924. His biographers write of him: 'He had no understanding of the ideas of the new socialism that people like James Connolly had . . .' ('Ní raibh aon dul amach aige ar smaointe nua-shóisialachais a bhí ag daoine cosúil le Séamas Ó Conghaile . . .') See Ó Conluain and Ó Céileachair, *An Duinníneach*, p. 233. For other examples of his thinking on

labour issues, see his columns in *The Leader* for 26 Aug., 2 Sept. and 30 Sept.
1911; 9 Mar. 1912; 18 Oct., 15 Nov. 1913; and 9 Feb. 1918. He was particularly
opposed to the use of sympathetic strikes during the Great Dublin Lockout of
1913 (as was Moran, for whom see *Leader*, 6 Sept. 1913).

35 Startlingly, he wrote of young women working in factories like this: 'It's
little wonder that today's young women are seeking to get the vote. Maybe
they'll have nothing as a result of the vote; but it's no wonder they are trying to
get some change in the life they are living' ('Is beag an iongnadh go bhfuil mná
óga an lae indiu ag iarraidh gothanna d'fhagháil. B'fhéidir ná beadh puinn de
bharra na ngothann aca; acht ni hiongnadh iad a bheith ag iarraidh athar-
ruighthe éigin ar an saoghal atá aca dá chaitheamh').

36 See, for example, his columns in *The Leader* for 23 Feb. 1907; 22 May 1909; 9
Dec. 1911; and 20 Dec. 1913. See also his highly idealised picture of the urban poor
in his *Leader* column for 14 Aug. 1926. Christmas often inspired him to write of
the poor. See also Ó Conluain and Ó Céileachair, *An Duinníneach*, p. 233.

37 See, for example, his columns in *The Leader* for 9 Dec. 1911; 1 Mar., 12 Apr.,
5 May. and 20 Dec. 1913. In his column for 18 Oct. 1913, written during the 1913
Lockout, he naively proposes labour-management cooperation as the solution
for the workers' job insecurity and poverty. He could, however, be sharply
critical of the callousness of the rich. See his columns for 28 June 1913; 9 Mar.
1918; and 9 Apr. 1927.

38 For links between suffragism and pacifism, see Owens, *Smashing Times*, p.
98; Rosemary Cullen Owens, 'Louie Bennett (1870–1956)', in *Female Activists*, p.
39; Murphy, *The Women's Suffrage Movement*, p. 73; Margaret Ward 'Nationalism,
pacifism, internationalism: Louie Bennett, Hannah Sheehy-Skeffington, and
the problems of 'Defining Feminism', in *Gender and Sexuality in Modern
Ireland*, Anthony Bradley and Maryann Gialanella Valiulis (eds) (Amherst,
1997), pp 60–84. See also 'The crime of war', Editorial, *IC*, 22 Aug 1914.

39 See, for example, his *Leader* columns for 3 Oct., 10 Oct., 17 Oct., 14 Nov., 28
Nov., and 19 Dec. 1914; 9 Jan., 3 July, 10 July, 17 July, 4 Sept., 18 Sept. and 25 Sept.
1915; 11 Mar. 1916; and 24 Feb. 1917.

40 See Mary Cullen (ed.), *Girls Don't do Honours: Irish Women in Education in
the 19th and 20th Centuries* (n.p. [Dublin,] 1987); Deirdre Raftery and Susan M.
Parkes, *Female Education in Ireland 1700–1900: Minerva or Madonna* (Dublin,
2007); and Medb Ruane, 'Kathleen Lynn', in *Female Acitivists*, pp 64–7. From his
days on the Coiste Gnó (Executive Committee) of the Gaelic League, Dinneen
had taken a dislike to his fellow committee member O'Farrelly. See Ó Conluain
and Ó Céileachair, *An Duinníneach*, p. 170. For O'Farrelly's involvement in the

[40 *cont.*] campaign for greater educational opportunities for women, see Ríona Nic Congáil, *Úna Ní Fhaircheallaigh agus an Fhís Útóipeach Ghaelach* (*Agnes O'Farrelly and the Gaelic Utopian Vision*) (Dublin, 2010), pp 158–96. Hayden would have angered Dinneen by her rejection of Catholic concerns about higher education for women in her testimony before a 1902 Royal Commission on third-level education for women. See Hearne, *The Development of Irish Feminist Thought*, pp 82–3; and Deirdre Raftery and Susan M. Parkes, *Female Education in Ireland 1700–1900: Minerva or Madonna* (Dublin, 2007), pp 120–2.

41 This article was prompted by Dinneen's reading about co-education in Canada in E. Way Elkington's *Canada: The Land of Hope* (London, 1910). Echoing his ideas in *The Queen of the Hearth*, Dinneen wrote of girls in this piece: 'They do not have the strength or the stamina to do heavy academic work and to continue that work for ten years or so . . . And what do they have for their work at last, after all the work? God and Mary help us, it is often very little, just lack of health and poverty' ('Ní bhíonn an neart ná an taitheach ionna [sic] chum obair throm scolaidheach do dhéanamh is leanamhain den obair sin ar feadh deich mbliadhan nó mar sin . . . Agus cad a bhíonn de bhárr a saothair aca fá dheireadh, tar éis na hoibre go léir? Dia linn is Muire, mhaise, is minic nach mór a bhíonn, acht easbaidh sláinte agus dealbhas').

42 He wrote of the judge: 'Six months for such delicate young girls! He might as well have have given them five years, or hanged them and been done with them' ('Leathbhliadhain do chailínibh óga leicthe dá leithéid! Bheadh sé chomh maith aige chúig bhliadhna do thabhairt dóibh, nó iad a chrochadh is bheith réidh leo').

43 After the 1917 death by force-feeding of the Republican rebel Thomas Ashe, Dinneen changed his mind entirely about the hunger strike, praising those male republican prisoners who used the tactic as patriots and martyrs. See his columns for 1 May, 16 Oct. and 30 Oct. 1920. In the first of these he praised the wives, mothers, and sisters of hunger strikers for supporting their men, writing: 'There is a spirit in the women of Ireland the like of which is not in any other race of women under the sun: they are women apart' ('Tá spiorad i mnáibh na hÉireann ná fuil a leithéid i n-aon treibh ban fán ngréin; bantracht fá leith is eadh iad').

44 It is worth comparing his perspective here to that of his fellow language revivalist Mary Butler in her 1900 Gaelic League pamphlet *Irishwomen and the Home Language*. Butler decried the activities of 'shrieking viragos or aggressive amazons', and, quoting Father Richard Henebry, called the hearth 'the

foundation of all true nationality', and urged Irish wives and mothers to do their duty to the Irish language: 'Their mission is to make the homes of Ireland Irish. If the homes are Irish, the whole country will be Irish. The spark struck on the hearthstone will fire the soul of the nation.' See also Máiréad Ní Chinnéide, *Máire de Buitléir: Bean Athbheochana* (*Mary Butler: A Woman of the Revival*) (Baile Átha Cliath, 1993), pp 79–84.

45 Not even his title was original. In her preface to *Women's Work* by Amy Bulley and Margaret Whitley (1894), Emilia Dilke argues that with regard to women's work, the goal of trade unionism was 'the restoration of as many as possible to their post of honour as queens of the hearth'. See Sandra Stanley Holton, *Feminism and Democracy: Women's Suffrage and Reform in Britain 1900–1918* (Cambridge, 1986), p. 25.

Perhaps we should not be too quick to blame him for his lack of originality, for, as David Morgan has noted, 'by the late 1880s, most of the arguments for and against Suffrage in principle and practice which were to be used until 1918 were already stock', Morgan, *Suffragists and Liberals*, pp 14–5. See also his biographers' opinion that Dinneen was neither an intellectual nor a deep thinker (Ó Conluain and Ó Céileachair, *An Duinníneach*, p. 254).

46 Quoted in Harrison, *Separate Spheres*, p. 37.

47 Interestingly enough, some suffragists developed their own version of this theory according to which women should be enfranchised precisely because of their presumed moral superiority and 'natural' domestic abilities, virtues that had to be given voice in the political realm. See Laura E. Nym Mayhall, *The Militant Suffrage Movement: Citizenship and Resistance in Britain, 1860–1930* (Oxford, 2003), pp 20–1; and Hearn, *The Development of Irish Feminist Thought*, pp 68–9, 204–5.

48 The editors at this time were Francis Sheehy-Skeffington and James Cousins. The term was coined by Margaret Cousins. Had Dinneen been aware of how she developed this idea through the use of Christian imagery he would have been even more shocked. See Catherine Candy, 'Margaret Cousins (1878–1954),' in Mary Cullen and Mary Luddy (eds), *Female Activists: Irish Women and Change 1900-1960* (Dublin, 2001), pp 116–8. See also Murphy, *The Women's Suffrage Movement*, p. 63; and Hearne, *The Development of Irish Feminist Thought*, pp 229–30.

Editorial Note

Dinneen wrote *The Queen of the Hearth* in pen on loose sheets of paper that he then clipped together into chapters. These chapters have obviously gotten shuffled with use in their folder in the National Library of Ireland, as the order in which they are presently filed does not match that of Dinneen's table of contents. For this edition, I have followed Dinneen's intended sequence. Some of the chapter headings on the manuscript pages do not exactly match those in the table of contents; I have used the latter. Dinneen's handwriting throughout is quite legible if never elegant, with only a handful of readings presenting even temporary difficulties. I was eventually able to decipher all but one of them. That problematic word, with my reading of it, is indicated in a note in the text. Dinneen's punctuation is inconsistent, and I have felt free to change it for the sake of clarity. In a very few places, I inserted a word that is obviously missing in the manuscript. Although a few of the pages present a rather chaotic appearance at first glance, Dinneen was actually quite clear about what he wanted to change, omit, or insert, as well as about where such insertions were to be placed. For this consideration on his part I am grateful to him and can only hope that he would have felt that this edition accurately conveys, if it cannot accept, ideas that were of considerable importance to him.

The Queen of the Hearth

✦

CHAPTER I

Introductory

One conspicuous result of the great world-war which came suddenly into existence in the beginning of August 1914 has been to put womankind in an unwonted and difficult position throughout the length and breadth of Europe.[1] In excess of the male population before the war they are far more numerous than them now. They have been subjected to hardships and privations innumerable, hunger and thirst, cold and fatigue, exhausting labour and bereavement, loneliness and sorrows, the husbands they loved, the sons they bore and cherished taken from them in their prime and sacrificed, in a foreign land for the most part, to an insatiable slaughter. They have had unwonted trials in patience and endurance, different in kind indeed from those of the soldiers at the battle-front, but in countless instances scarcely less searching or intense. The loved ones died but once in the field of blood; wife and sister and mother have felt a thousand times pangs more bitter than death through anxiety and foreboding. In imagination they have been witnesses of the bloodiest engagements; and plains sheeted with blood have expanded before their eyes. They have gone down into the cold, dismal trenches to witness the agony and torture of the wounded and dying.

These sufferings have not indeed been unmingled with consolations and these consolations are common to victors and vanquished.

Tales of heroism in the field, of patience in privation and sorrow, of brotherly love and a large-hearted charity that embraced the enemy, have illumined every phase of the mighty struggle and served to brighten many a desolate home. The virtues that in peaceful times ripen slowly and diffuse a steady fragrance around now burst forth with amazing suddenness into brilliant and deathless deeds. The women at home have shared in the glory, and most of all the mothers of the heroes whose exploits and self-sacrifice have been as a bright sunshine gilding the clouds that have so long settled on the face of Europe. Who shall say what the mother of a soldier hero feels when there comes to her news of a death crowning deeds that will never die? Who does not envy that mother the very flesh of whose flesh has become sacred clay consecrated to heroism and to duty? The cruel war has made many a woman the mother of a hero whose exploits will ring through generations yet to rise. It has been a war in which the leaders though faithful to duty have nevertheless yielded the palm of distinguished merit to the privates and non-commissioned.

Among the great wars in the world's story it is eminent as the war of the common soldier, of the young man who, in many instances, coming almost directly from the plough, the counter, the factory, the hall of learning, his mother's parting advice and blessing still echoing in his heart, rushes into the maze of battle and lays down his young life on the sacred altar of what he considers his duty to God and to his kith and kin. Bitter and overwhelming will be that mother's grief, but hers will be the proud privilege of having lived to see exemplified in the life, and especially in the death, of her son those principles of honour, of unselfish sacrifice with which she charged his boyish mind.

It is not often given to a wide circle of women to witness the blossoming of the principles they have inculcated into deeds of honour and renown; to have the soundness of their teaching, the thoroughness of their training of their sons tried and approved in fields of slaughter. This has been the glory of the present generation. This has emphasised the significance of motherhood, its duties, its responsibilities, its opportunities. This has given a new direction and a new meaning to the question of woman's duties and woman's rights. From it we may learn the paramount importance of good and early training, and of the strengthening of family ties; from it we learn to appreciate more justly than heretofore the enthusiasm which the name of mother evokes. That name is a battle-cry which has a special and most sacred meaning for each individual soldier and that is capable of inciting to deeds of imperishable renown. It links the hearth, warm, homely, peaceful, with the trench in the battled plain putrid with corpses and drenched in blood.

The great European contest has brought about a change in the occupation of women. A considerable number have been employed as nurses to the wounded in the various hospitals and have been afforded a unique opportunity of exercising the virtues of patience and self-sacrifice as well as of becoming familiar with human sorrow and suffering in some of their acutest phases. Nursing, however, on such an extensive scale must necessarily be but of short duration, and the nurses whose vigilant attention the soldiers no longer require will carry their experience and skill and tenderness into the great ravaged world outside. There are, however, many occupations less congenial to women than nursing and normally suitable only for men in which women have been employed during the war. It may be assumed that they will retain these posts for a considerable time after the signing of peace, and in many instances, that they will retain them indefinitely There are certain posts, however, such as those immediately connected with locomotives or foundries, which though they may be filled by women in an emergency are quite unsuitable for them as permanent work, while the great war has brought into the clearest light the intrinsic value of the due discharge of their own essential duties. No doubt a period of, say, ten years of peace and re-construction will go far to restore an equilibrium of occupations as between the sexes. In any event the problem of a great and unprecedented excess of unmarried women and widows will press for solution in the years immediately before us. The trials and sufferings undergone by them in the course of the mighty contest will stand them in stead in the work of repairing and renovating the social fabric.

As is pointed out in these pages, unmarried women – and we may add with due qualification, childless widows – have an exalted mission to fulfill, and it would be to the detriment to human society if to any serious extent their energies were devoted to work for which they are unsuited to the neglect of the essential business of their lives. The time is at hand when their peculiar virtues will be a priceless asset in the treasury of a restored and rejuvenated social system. By their courage, patience and cheerfulness, by their sympathy with suffering of every description, by their heroic immolation of themselves and of their own interests for the welfare of others, they can do invaluable work in lifting human society from the slough of depression and desolation into which the war has sunk it. It will be their special task to minister to the poor, the homeless, the orphans, the sick, and the dying; to knit together the torn fabric of domestic life. They will indeed have trials of their own; will suffer privations and hardships; will be often slighted and despised; but the time of stress through which they will have lived will have prepared them for burthens such as these.

It would seem as if on tragic occasions such as the present the world needed the special assistance of such a sympathetic and unselfish host to minister to the sore needs of humanity. Who so well as unmarried women can nurse the sick, attend to the wants of the tender orphan, help the maimed and poverty-stricken, console the dying? Who so well suited as these angels of self-immolation and innocence to restore to the world, weary and enervated from war, its wonted gaiety, its self-reliance, its hope in the future? The soldiers have spent months busied in the work of destroying human life, property and time-honoured monuments, as if in frenzied agony they were bent on effacing from the earth every vestige of humanity. And when the bloody work has at length ceased there arises an army of a different kind, a host of virgins armed with weapons very dissimilar to those of the agents of destruction, ready to build up the shattered frame of human society; a host that will firmly plant in the new world on which we are entering the saving virtues of patience, sympathy with suffering, forgetfulness of self, in their desire to minister to those in need – and while not participating in the physical perpetuation of the human race, will still devote their energies to the work of moulding it in spirit and in hope. The work which the exigencies of the time demand from this noble host will bear comparison with that accomplished by their brothers in the trenched field. It is no less noble, and hardly less important. It is more silent and less ostentatious. Instead of arresting the flow of commerce or the wheels of industry, it promotes and stimulates every useful occupation; instead of converting wide plains into crowded graveyards, it seeks to prolong life and to rescue from death many on whom neglect and disease had laid heavy hands. Their trenches are the hospitals, the homes of the poor, the lairs of the outcasts of society; their bivouac the dens of disease where humanity is prostrate in suffering; their prisoners wretches snatched from sin and shame; their conquests areas where poverty in squalid state has been presiding over the physical and moral degradation of thousands.

The war has brought into prominence how necessary to safeguard a state is an abundance of energetic, obedient men, and has demonstrated clearly the dignity and importance of the maternal office. It has laid special emphasis on the duties and privileges of those women who are destined to live in the married state and become mothers. It has proved even to the blindest the necessity of a healthy and sufficiently numerous population inhabiting every tract of country worth defending against invaders. Whatever progress may be made in the development of machinery or of engines of destruction, fighting members will never be superseded as a decisive force in offensive or defensive warfare. But mere numbers are insufficient. There must be sound physical training and upbringing in a healthy moral atmosphere. It is obvious that there cannot be a sufficient population to supply fighting men in such circumstances where motherhood does not receive due recognition and where the maternal duties are not modeled on high ideals. The mother makes the soldier as she makes the professional man and the legislator. Her empire is all-embracing; she is in charge of the entire human race, especially during its most impressionable stage of development. Her importance is to be measured not alone by great armies in the clash of battle but by all the varied activities that go to the making of human society. In the forum, in the senate, in the municipal committee room, in the noisy factory, in the peaceful pasturage, on land and sea, the seed she sows in young and pliant minds will produce fruit after its kind, good or evil. A great army is a close and searching test of the strength of a state. It is the weakest link that snaps, but the entire chain of defence or offence is no stronger, and every link in the chain of state-strength directly or indirectly derives its force from maternity. There are indeed other tests of a state's strength besides war A state may sink never to rise again in time of the calmest peace. Corruption in public and private life, the decay of morals, the prevalence of enervating habits, forces such as these are capable of crippling even the most powerful states and of rendering them an easy prey to covetous neighbours or of involving them for generations in the turmoil of confusion and anarchy. On the other hand, the spirit of self-sacrifice, of loyalty to kith and kin and country, of love of rational liberty, of hatred of injustice, will buoy up a weak state and will to no unimportant extent supply for deficiencies in numbers and in war materials.

Although during or immediately after a war women may claim the right to be employed in certain posts usually filled by men, it may be said in general that the great European conflict has pointed out with emphasis some broad line of demarcation between the pursuits that are most suitable for the sexes. The active career of the soldier including military training is out for the weaker vessels. But this career postulates in a well-ordered state a youth inured to toil and practised in every manly exercise. The education and upbringing of boys and girls should therefore proceed on different lines and serious attempts at ignoring their differences of habits, their unequal capacities of mind and body, in the educational and industrial fields, must lead to disaster.

While skill and efficiency in war are necessary for a nation's well-being, these cannot stand alone, but must be associated with legislative, administrative, diplomatic and financial ability and training. War is a severe and relentless and often an unexpected test of a people's physical and moral development and lays its unerring hands on the blots of national degeneracy and debasement. It distinguishes unmistakably real from counterfeit public virtue, real from counterfeit national progress, and from its decisions there is no appeal. Wars great and little are certain to come and woe to the nation they find unprepared. But true preparedness for war implies far more than the drilling and arming of as large a number of men as possible; it implies the leavening of the whole nation with the principles of truth, justice, self-sacrifice and self-reliance; it implies the training of the young in sobriety and honesty, in love of home and country; and it is in the mother's own school, the fundamental school of the human race, that such training must originate and strike deep root, and it is the mother who is intended by nature to plant and to water it.

While the world still rocks with the force of a mighty conflict, it may not be inopportune to study that element in human society which is so potent a factor in its evolution and on which so much will depend in the work of restoring equilibrium to the disturbed condition of social order.[2]

CHAPTER 2

Woman and the Hearth

Old institutions are falling into ruins around us before the new ones have had time to rise and take firm root. Certain vague things, full of half-veiled terrors, called Socialism and Syndicalism are lifting their heads and struggling to find expression and lisping things scarcely heard before. The lisp may become a loud voice and re-echo from end to end of the world. The Constitutions of the great European nations have been undergoing a severe strain in these latter fateful years, and even the British Constitution that has weathered so many storms shows signs of yielding to extreme pressure. Of the three constituent parts of the latter constitution one has already given way before the battering-ram of radicalism. It has thrown open its doors and given up its keys.[3] Another is still in nominal possession but its power is a thing of the past.[4] To the third part, the Commons, then, belongs everything that remains of governmental power. It has the first and last word in legislation and administration, in the affairs of war and peace, of expenditure and taxation, of education, of industrial development, of social order, of foreign policy, of domestic discipline. But the institution of the Commons is itself fast yielding to the stress of modern ideas. It is no longer the old institution though it bear the ancient name. Irish Home Rule legislation has scarred it deeply. Its individual members though well-paid have but little power. Its business is managed for it by a small body called a Cabinet which in its turn is dominated by a few men.

The parliamentary[5] franchise though confined to men is already framed on a wide basis. Yet there is a serious movement to extend it to women, at least to women who own a certain amount of property; and woman franchise in this restricted sense has solid support from members of Parliament of all parties. An active campaign by a band[6] of militant women in favour of a restricted suffrage for their sex was in full vigour when the great war broke out and will no doubt be revived on the establishment of peace. There is reason to believe however that the great majority of women were not in sympathy with the violent methods of that campaign and even that a large proportion of adult women are not anxious to become parliamentary voters. But the agitation has had the result of drawing attention to the position of women in modern life and earnest minds are endeavouring to solve the problems which it presents. They are striving to discover how women are to fare in the new order of things, what is to be their status in the new world of which we can as yet obtain but shadowy glimpses.[7]

The real question as regards the position of women is not whether they are to be parliamentary voters. They may have votes and yet get ground to dust by a tyranny against which they are powerless. They may find the fabric of social life drifting in a certain inevitable direction and forcing them along to slavery and degradation without being able to help themselves. On the other hand, even without the parliamentary vote they may succeed by active propaganda in impressing their peculiar wants on the legislature and the public. Men are quite capable of understanding their difficulties and hardships and peculiar needs and are willing to redress their grievances provided they are brought before them with sufficient force and clearness and that other matters they may deem of greater urgency and importance do not stand in the way. But the woman problem should not be regarded as existing by itself as if the women of the world were a separate race held in bondage by a tyrannous people called men. They are not a separate race. The tyrannous race of men would be inconceivable without them. Their interests are indissolubly linked with those of men. Every triumph won by men is a triumph of a father, son, brother or husband actual or prospective. No assembly of fathers, sons, husbands, brothers would deliberately plan laws to oppress their daughters, wives, sisters, mothers, though they may through forgetfulness or neglect allow their grievances to go unredressed. So closely linked are the interests of women with those of their husbands, brothers, sons, that no legislature can ever tear them asunder. The condition of women in the workaday and social world may[8] undergo a change under the stress of advanced[9] legislation, but they shall ever be the sisters, wives, mothers, daughters of the legislators and subjects. Laws may be introduced making household management more complex, restricting the authority of the husband, hedging the wife round with protection and making the children in a certain measure independent of their parents and dependent on the state,[10] but in spite of the way in which domestic conjugal life will be modified[11] by such legislation, the conjugal and maternal instincts of womankind will assert themselves. No matter what legislation may devise, domestic life is the highest ideal of their happiness as daughters and sisters in the first stage, in the next as wives and mothers, and as all cannot become wives and as a certain proportion elect a single life, as sisters and daughters still, and in the third stage as mothers of adult sons and daughters and as grandmothers.

The hearth is their sphere of life, the theatre of their joys and triumphs. Nature has planted in their souls an instinct which never gets its full satisfaction outside the sacred precincts of home life. Men cannot live without a hearth. Even the tribes that roam from place to place pitching their tents as convenience suggests, carry their home life with them and cherish it as a sacred treasure. No hearth, no home, is complete without a woman. Her withdrawal even for a week or a day brings gloom and desolation on the house. Her total withdrawal by death or otherwise creates a state of things which may be endured in isolated cases but which if it became general would make of human life a state of joyless bondage.[12]

The hearth, then, is the centre of the happiness, the life, the activity of womankind. The mother at her own fireside is a noble type[13] of womanhood. She fills a position which women in general are instinctively aiming at as a crowning happiness. Her children are growing up around her, some mere infants, some approaching adult age. From her place at the fireside she watches their career at home, at school, or mingling with the busy throng of the great world. She follows her husband's part in the drama of human life with a devotion and unselfish interest. Her influence is felt everywhere; at the meeting where her husband speaks, at the entertainment where her sons and daughters assemble. She directs all, draws all to her rules. All is gentleness and sweetness; and yet does not for one instant compromise the dignity of womanhood. By her power over her husband and sons as well as over male relatives and friends, she may influence important elections and play no inconsiderable part in public affairs; but all this she does in that quiet, tactful, graceful fashion which is part of the secret of her power. The same person may be imagined under a new dispensation standing on a public platform and laying down public policy amongst male speakers and addressing an audience for the most part male. There are some women in every age who can occupy a public platform with dignity. But in general the atmosphere that surrounds a platform is uncongenial to the female character.[14] Woman, often endowed with[15] close connected reasoning power and high eloquence, for the most part advocates her policy on the public stage in pointless and unconvincing speeches. But in her pulpit on the hearth she is irresistible. Here there is no inducement to weigh arguments in the cold scales of logic nor to affect the swelling periods, the lofty indignation, the glowing rhetoric of the orator. Her presence, her demeanour, her winning graces, her smile of approval, her look of displeasure, her sigh half expressing half concealing a depth of feeling, are infinitely more eloquent and persuasive than her studied efforts on the platform. The power of eloquent persuasion which woman possesses in her native sphere is a natural asset of her sex of which no one can deprive her except herself, and is higher in degree and quality than any derived from the platform or the polling-booth. A woman at her own fireside, turning into best account her womanly graces and attractions and bringing into play all the advantages of her position is moving in her sphere of greatest dignity and power. She is as it were a throned monarch. Her every word is law. The slightest indication of her wishes is a command. Men make themselves the willing slaves of her attractions.[16] Her opinion even on abstruse questions is eagerly sought and esteemed of high value. She is powerful to lead, direct, persuade. But change the scene. Plant her on a platform. Let her speak on public questions, discuss public policy, answer arguments, make appeals, deliver invectives. Here she takes her place amongst men, she has to reply to them and defend her position, weigh and sift evidence and with vehemence exhort or dissuade. Her best efforts are discounted, her logic is criticised, her rhetoric received with coldness, her facts submitted to a close examination. When she grows passionate she moves the audience to ridicule; her anger is a cause of laughter. Even the speeches of pretty and amiable women fall flat on the public ear. There is a deep and ineradicable feeling in the human heart hostile to the discussion of public questions or the management of public affairs by females.

In a theatre, acting a woman's part in a play or singing in a concert, a woman breathes something of the atmosphere of the fireside.[17] If she has histrionic power together with grace and beauty she carries all before her. She is queen and victor and idol all in one, but here she is not relying on her logic or on her capacity for public business, she is simply displaying her domestic qualities according to approved rules of art. The sphere in which actresses and singers move is the just domain of woman where she may reign and triumph and display her talents to the best advantage. Actresses and singers are exposed to dangers and cruel temptations, and require safeguards and protections, but the duties on which they are engaged are in a certain sense congenial to the constitution and capacity of their sex. It would however be absurd to say that women should never appear on a public platform as speakers or ever undertake transaction of public affairs. I am not dealing with special cases in which such action would be excusable and most effective. The special circumstances and the corresponding demeanour of the women would disarm criticism. In such cases she carries with her on the platform the atmosphere of the home. It is a call of duty or necessity that brings her forward. She is placed in a position which necessitates public speaking or the conduct of public affairs. Men loyally and gallantly accept the situation and the woman rules and triumphs. But exceptions such as these do not make an universal law; they are only apparent exceptions to the rule that the hearth and not the public platform is the proper sphere of woman's labours and the proper scene of her triumphs. It will be said that women may retain their domesticity and still do their duty to the state by voting for members of Parliament.[18] If it were merely a question of the periodic recording of votes it is difficult to see how the domestic character of women would suffer thereby. Indeed such are the laws that govern property and taxes in the United Kingdom that women who possess property have a claim[19] to the franchise. We must, however, regard the parliamentary franchise as a step in a direction full of danger and which it would be difficult to retrace. It must lead to canvassing, public meetings, public speaking, long journeys, revision conferences. It must lead to courses of public action which may be trusted to give a freer rein to passions which as far as women are concerned had better be kept in check and will act as a hindrance to the legitimate exercise by them of the powers of persuasion and eloquence with which they are endowed and of which the hearth is the natural sphere.

Woman warms the hearth by the fervour of her spirit. She grows chill in the atmosphere of Parliament or the polling booth. She adorns the hearth with her graces and her virtues, these graces and these virtues are strangely out of place in regions of the stress of deliberation and the strife of debate. She is the queen of the hearth, but a perturbed and perturbing spirit in the arena of public debate.

CHAPTER 3

Woman's Work

The hearth as we have seen is the natural and legitimate sphere of woman's activities whether she be married or single; and the men she can most influence are those who naturally gravitate thither. Those who are connected with her by social or domestic ties rather than general masses of mankind such as may be reached from public platforms. The hearth being the true sphere of her energies, it follows that the kind of work most suitable for her is the work that has the hearth for its basis, household or domestic work, everything connected with the arrangement and setting in order of the house.[20] It is the woman's province to prepare food for the family circle and this involves a series of occupations intimately associated with the hearth with or without the aid of subordinates.[21] She should not be engaged in occupations that afford no leisure for occasional lapses in strength. To speak generally, rough toilsome work requiring great physical strength, either in the open air or under cover such as work in forges, foundries, laboratories should be left to men. As regards work in offices clerical and other, custom has given sanction to her employment in such positions and her work may be rendered more endurable in them by improved conditions. Work of administration such as that of judges, magistrates, law officers, juries,[22] attorneys, barristers is in general outside her range.[23] Women are not in their true element as brokers, money-changers, bank clerks, and it is plain that the work of soldiers, sailors, policemen, bailiffs, porters, drivers is uncongenial to their constitution and character as well as repugnant to their tastes. They shrink naturally and constitutionally from occupations that bring them in contact with the rough world outside, from work in which they have to do with large masses of persons otherwise unknown to them, from work requiring late hours and public soli-tariness, from work requiring great bodily strength, from work requiring continuous vigour over a period of years and giving no leisure for occasional indisposition. Learned professions may attract some women by their dignity and exclusiveness, but they will never please the many nor will the many be ever likely to prove equal to their demands. The work of nursing the sick though difficult and exacting and requiring much patience and endurance is nothing more than a domestic duty even when performed in hospitals and is congenial to a woman's nature.

If we had an ideal state of female employment, home life would be steeped in happiness. There we should behold mother and daughters with or without the assistance of maids, engaged from morning till night in the congenial work of making domestic life comfortable and happy for their menfolk and for themselves. The labours of even an humbler household are multifarious and vary in kind with the variations of successive civilizations, but in their essence they are the same in every age and a division of labour between the mother and her daughters and helpers serves to lighten their work. One has charge of the cooking and reigns in the kitchen, no mean realm to be queen in; another superintends the wardrobe, a department that demands care and skill and that is ever giving surprises and excitement by reason of the changes in fashion; a third is responsible for the dining room and all that it implies; a fourth specialises in all that belongs to entertainments, music, singing; a fifth sees to the marketing and so on. Their occupations will vary with circumstances, but the poorest home will repay careful attention and diligent service. All are happy. Many kinds of work may be done in common and the labour lightened by pleasant companionship. The mother or eldest daughter will naturally preside over the various centres of activity and all will feel the pleasure of being employed in useful home work under the direction of a kind and loving taskmaster. A happy home is a state of ideal bliss in this life at which so many are aiming, but which is seldom attained in any approach to perfection.

The more thoroughly womankind set about the work of adorning, preserving and furnishing the home the happier will home life be. How blissful is a day of quiet healthful labour, the men occupied out of doors in city or country, the women engaged in the house or in its environs and mingling pleasant conversation with their work. They are engaged in occupations congenial to their nature and which lay no severe tax on their strength. They work under favourable conditions. Their taskmaster is their own mother or an elder sister. If they are fatigued they are allowed to rest. If they require a change of work it is granted to them. If they wish to go into the town it can be so arranged. They feel they are working for their own immediate family and for themselves. For have they not a claim on the family assets, and is it not a claim that will be readily acceded to? The work may be hard upon occasion but there are periods of rest. There are leisure hours. There is time for dressing, for the ornamentation of the person, for visits to friends, for making fresh acquaintances. There is the quiet restful evening when the brothers and father join the family. There is the evening meal in common. There is conversation, calm, pleasant and soothing, in which the events of the day are recorded and discussed. A book or paper is read, a story told, a neighbour drops in to gossip, plans are laid for the coming day. There is a calmness and peace in the atmosphere that money cannot buy. There is talk of the coming public entertainment if one lives in the country or of some corresponding events if in town, the vision of new dresses and new acquaintances that it calls up, the hopes that it enkindles; in anticipation they are already treading the street flags dressed in the fashion and going forward to conquest. There are entertainments, a dance, singing. Friends and neighbours are present. The air is charged with the electricity of pleasurable feeling and no sleep till morn. The preparations have been made for the wedding or for the christening, the gowns that have to be provided, the hats with their trimming, all in the newest fashion, the curtains have to be washed, the carpets beaten and the dining room papered and set with new tables and chairs. Strangers from a distance will be present and cousins and uncles and aunts. Everything must be in good order and the house must look its best. Every month, almost every week, brings some new task, some fresh excitement, new calls for labour, new sensations of parties, new hopes, new feverish longings, and thus the year marches on with ever new prospects, some fulfilled, some blighted, but with a consistent flow of happiness and with unvarying contentment. Year succeeds year in this blissful state, the wedding, the christening, the re-union of friends, the day of the sports or the races, the fair day, etc. being landmarks.

In spite of arduous work the kind domestic discipline secures that not only is good health safeguarded but a fund of animal spirits is maintained which makes life pleasant and gives a keen relish for the good things it affords. The thought of working for one's own family and for one's self robs fatiguing labour of its terrors and invests with interest even the dullest occupation. The maid-servant in a well-regulated house feels at home, looks upon herself as a member of the family and shares in the privileges of the household, and no household can be considered well-regulated that does not make liberal provision for the comfort and happiness of those who do its work but are for the time removed from their parents' care.

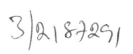

How a woman's heart goes out to the happy home where she reigns as queen, where there are no suspicions or misunderstandings, no dread of impending calamities, no danger of dismissal from service, where everything is taken in good part, and an eternal contract sealed with heart's kisses is in no danger of being set aside, where every desire of the human breast is satisfied, and all that is sweet in life is sweetest, all that is lovely is loveliest; where affection blunts the arrows of adversity and the wine of life is purest and most exhilarating and the bitterest sorrow is sweetened by sympathy, where the heart's language wells up spontaneously from the lips[24] and there is no pretence, no false zeal, no counterfeit affection; where love is genuine and grief unfeigned, where misfortunes and burthens are lightest and joy is the brightest. Here the woman reigns as queen and mother; her power is undisputed, her authority is not limited by the cold letter of law or contract. The instinct of obedience to her decrees is planted by nature in the hearts of her children. Obedience is a cold dull word to describe the flaming zeal and ardent devotion with which her every wish is carried out. Her heart beats again in the hearts of her offspring, her thoughts find an echo in their minds. They are pledges that bind her to life. They are guarantees of happiness, titles[25] to remembrance, objects on which nature's treasury of affection may be liberally bestowed and which will as liberally return it. A mother exercises a power over her offspring in controlling the springs of affection, of sympathy, of devotion within them such as is given to none other. Money, titles, honours, the glory of a great name are powerless to command the chivalrous loyalty, the unswerving love which the poorest and most desolate of mothers claims as her due. There is no bitterness in a mother's anger, there is no harshness in her voice, her reproof is soft and gentle, her approbation thrills, her smile is a glimpse of paradise. What human happiness can equal the happiness of the home where the mothers and daughters work together for the general comfort, where the interests of the menfolk are ever present to their minds and they find that in consulting their happiness they are treading the paths of happiness themselves. They are no slaves but as it were partners in the firm. The part they take is that which fits in with their powers and is dictated by their instincts. They can but ill fit any other part. It is a part which satisfies all their longings and that calls out their best endeavour and which honestly filled affords a supreme measure of human happiness.[26] But if it be neglected through the spread of false notions of the true position of women, the loss to the family, to woman herself, and to the human race will be great. Womankind need not go outside the region of the hearth to find complete happiness. Every happy home in a village or district radiates its happiness all round and increases that of its neighbours. By increasing the number of happy homes we raise the town or district to a more exalted life. The happiness enjoyed by a locality may be said to be directly proportional to the fidelity with which the womenfolk interpret their mission.

CHAPTER 4

The Education of Women

The occupations of women, the sphere worked out for them in life, their mental endowments and physical constitution should rule their education. In every practical system, however, there must be allowed a large margin for education not considered exactly as such but as an ancillary to employment. In modern times many of the posts that women fill have little in them to interest feminine nature. They are hard, monotonous, dull, but women are so extensively employed in these posts that there is an active demand for a system of education enabling them to obtain them, often by competitive examinations, and to acquit themselves in them with success they must be assiduously coached in arithmetic, in geography, in précis, in composition, in spelling. The course is limited in time. Up to a certain age,[27] they are eligible; beyond that age they cannot compete. No allowance is made for family circumstances, for constitutionally slow development, for visitations of sickness, for the distraction of sudden calamities.

The competition for public and semipublic posts pits country against city girls, the robust against those of weak health, the precocious against those of slower development, the clever against the dull. The strain of such a system is severe. Its results are often disastrous both as regards those who fail and those who succeed.

Success in obtaining a place is dearly bought at the expense of health and vigour. The system is perhaps a necessary evil of our time, and our efforts should be directed to the work of improving it. We are concerned here with the spirit which should direct female education, and which though powerless to control its details, or to shield it from the aggressive commercialism of the age, will, still, be of service in regulating general principles which in any age cannot be disregarded with impunity.

Women, then, are by nature destined for home life, to act as companions to men, and take charge of domestic affairs.[28] It is their office to bring into the world children of both sexes, and to nurse and rear them and watch over them during their tender years and bear no light part of the responsibility of settling them in life. Not all women are destined to become wives and mothers, but many of those who live singly are called upon to take an active part in the work of rearing and training children, of nursing the sick, in the various offices of household management. They have to act as cooks, nurses, housemaids, governesses, children's maids, housekeepers. Even more external works in which women are wont to be employed or which are suitable for them savour of domestic life and of its peculiar duties.

The typical woman, however, is the mother, and it is the functions and requirements of motherhood that should in the main regulate the course of education. On behalf of the future human race, men and women of the future, we may justly claim that the mother who brings them forth, who nurses them in infancy, who protects their childhood, who feeds their young minds with principles of religion and morals which are wont to make a deep impression,[29] whose duty it is to settle them in life, whose honour they are destined to hold dear, for whom they will cherish an affection having its roots deep in their nature, whose very name is the tenderest sound their tongue can utter, we may justly claim that her education shall not be at variance with her duties, that if human education do not improve her God-given qualities, at least it shall not impair or thwart nature.

Education is a means to an end. It is not something of itself absolutely necessary. Girls have by nature no slight share of the benefits which education is expected to confer. They are naturally refined, gentle, compassionate, sympathetic. A system of education that will not strengthen these qualities, but will rather tend to root them out, is a great evil and tends to bring those who receive it below nature's level. Education will not leave women as it found them. It will either raise or lower them. It cannot raise them except in so far as it fits them for their obvious duties; though it may have high-sounding names to recommend it, they must necessarily be lowered by it, and they cannot be lowered without dragging down with them the entire race.

Of the many qualities which female education should foster instead of destroying we may put in the first place womanliness, or female reserve and modesty. It is not necessary to describe here the girl or grown woman who has lost that heaven-given characteristic. It is the salt of her sex; and its flavour once lost cannot be restored to it. It distinguishes women more than dress or beauty, more than learning or accomplishments. It is something without which they are an unspeakable horror in the household – a source of anxiety, and even of shame, to their parents if grown up girls, an object of disgust to the world if adults, if mothers a source of danger and calamity to the rising generation. Whatever element in the education of girls, then, tends to remove or even to diminish this priceless quality should be eliminated.

The education of girls and boys or young men in the same schools, in the same halls, and in the same classes, and in the same curriculum, is a fruitful cause of the decay of this natural modesty amongst women. This coeducation, as it is called, should be avoided except in cases of necessity; and even in such cases certain obvious measures should be taken to obviate some of its evils.[30] Girls develop much more rapidly than boys, and both are unequal pupils at a given age. They are quicker than boys in some respects, and slower in others. Their physical constitution unfits them for the serious work of competing with boys. If they sometimes try to do so and succeed, it is at very great cost, and because it is a characteristic of theirs to suffer in silence and without complaint.

Some women who are clamouring for independence fondly imagine co-education to be an important step in the march to that goal. Alas, coeducation often entails a silent slavery more injurious to the physical and mental health of girls than any ever denounced by the philanthropist. Girls enjoy the society of their brothers and near male relatives. They are at their ease in their presence. They derive advantage from their acquaintance and vice-versa. On occasion they may profit by the society, under due restraint, of other boys of their own or their brothers' acquaintance. But there is a certain natural reserve on their part which lends a charm to their presence. Their time is limited. The freedom they allow themselves is restricted. They come as a dream and memories of them haunt their friends when they disappear. There is an atmosphere of romance and mystery about them which reserve but fosters. Their dress, their complexion, their bearing, even the colour of their eyes, are but half revealed half speculated on, and in part dreamt about by their young male friends, and imagination supplies many a glowing tint.

The school-halls and class-rooms are not peopled by heroes or knights of chivalry or princes of fairyland, by queens, angels or goddesses. Girls who have to go through the dull routine of a school-day cannot be always in their best looks or on their best behaviour. They must leave their romance behind them at home, if they be romantic even there. They appear to their male schoolmates as the weak, silly, vain, unlovely creatures that they will often be in unguarded conjunctures, and they are looked down on by them accordingly. They know too soon things that should reveal themselves to them but gradually. They grow up without the sacred halo of romance or womanly mystery that is at once a safeguard and an asset for their sex; and life begins to unfold to them its ugly unpoetic side long before the golden time of marriage. A girl issues from a co-educating school much less a girl than she entered it. She is drawn half-unconsciously to ape boys' ways, to adopt their language, to play their pranks, to imitate their example. She succeeds but ill in acting their part; meantime her native womanliness has become blunter, and she grows up without the strength or vigour of a man, and without the grace and charm of a woman. One shudders at the prospect of such women becoming mothers and nurses of the future race. If girls grow up in unwomanly habits they will find their maternal instincts blunted, those maternal instincts that are the foundation of those very qualities that make woman a desirable companion for man and enable her to fulfill her functions in the growth of the human family.

The coming race of men have sore need of womanliness and motherliness in their future wives and mothers. It is the function of education to strengthen these characteristics, and when it fails in this, when it weakens and tends to efface them instead, it becomes a curse rather than a blessing. Coeducation is detrimental[31] no less in the higher or university classes than in the elementary ones. As the curriculum grows in difficulty, girls find the strain the greater, and the uselessness of much of what they are endeavouring to learn the more apparent. There is naturally greater freedom allowed to girls in the higher classes. It is the most impressionable time of their lives and yet they are permitted to consort in large numbers[32] with male fellow-students, to contract secret acquaintances and

friendships without adequate protection or safeguard. Familiarities
of this nature cannot take place without serious risk; they tend to
unsettle the minds of the girl students and unfit them for immediate
and future work. Their presence, too, in the lecture hall is in some[33]
instances embarrassing to the professors, and detrimental to the
progress of serious work. University professors feel embarrassed
when lecturing to mixed audiences on certain subjects[34] which
cannot be treated of in the circumstances with reasonable thoroughness except by creating an atmosphere charged with indelicacy. In
the majority[35] of the subjects that find a place in the higher programme, girls though straining themselves to the utmost are a clog
on the wheels of progress; and male students however much some of
them may enjoy their society, often[36] resent their intrusion into the
arena of their studious labours. In the medical course their presence
is disconcerting in the last degree. Nowadays girls go up for university degrees and such like distinctions in large numbers. If we
consider the amount of mental strain a degree course entails on a girl
student we shall not be surprised at so many of our girls breaking
down early in health and becoming a burthen to their parents.

It is too often forgotten that strength of nerve and brain power
are necessary not only for the acquisition of knowledge and going
through an educational course, but also and in a greater degree for
the use of acquired knowledge and of acquired mental habits in
fighting the battle of life. The forced education of the modern
school has not even the compensation of an adequate material
reward. Many of its victims not only receive no recompense for
their activities but have to engage in the commerce of life bankrupt
in health and strength, their minds and bodies enfeebled and a prey
to disease. Periodic headaches, disorders of the eyes, constipation,
cerebrasthenia,[37] epilepsy, hysteria, weak resistance to epidemics,
proneness to tuberculosis are some of the results of the high

pressure at which the education of modern youth of both sexes is proceeding around us. But this pressure produces its most patent and disastrous results in the case of females.

Women are not intended by nature for the prolonged study of serious subjects and if they violate nature's laws they must pay the penalty. Not only is the University course long and taxing and difficult, but the subjects are for the most part uncongenial. Outside of a limited number of subjects[38] almost every subject in the University curriculum has to be studied by girls against the grain, and their diligence in such studies is seldom rewarded by distinction. A girl student rarely distinguishes herself in higher mathematics.[39] For most girls mathematics is useless, a difficult and an uninteresting study. Girls as a rule do not attain eminence as classical scholars.[40] They are not often distinguished[41] in logic and philosophy; they are left behind[42] in physical and natural sciences. They succeed to a remarkable degree[43] in the vernacular and in modern languages and in certain other courses. Their tastes incline them to succeed in cultivated modern tongues, not from a philological standpoint but rather as writers and speakers. Why are they tortured in mind and body with the study of weighty subjects for which they have but little aptitude, and less inclination, and which when mastered are but useless lumber in their heads? Can it be a healthy exercise for future mothers to wear out the bloom of their lives in the study of Conic Sections, of Kantian Philosophy, of the Greek Drama, of biological theories, of zoological specimens? We know that they will but rarely distinguish themselves in such courses, that they are uncongenial to their tastes, while they tax their constitution to the utmost, that they turn away their energies from their natural channel.

And what benefit will they themselves or the future race derive from this straining of mind and nerve? Fresh discoveries in science, classical scholarship of a high order? New light on philosophical

problems? Results like these are seldom likely to ensue. What benefits, then, may be expected from such violence to nature? Congenial
and secure livelihood? Would it were so. Girls, however, are not in
demand as teachers of those subjects they strain themselves to
master. A female teacher's income is precarious and will seldom be
the higher for her abstruse studies. The energies thus wasted on
useless and uncongenial studies might have indeed developed the
girl's mind in its proper course, might have helped to settle her in
life in some congenial sphere and to give to a future progeny a
mother who has her natural faculties strengthened and developed,
and her maternal instincts preserved from adverse influences.[44]

When abstruse studies are seriously undertaken by girls, they
do not fail to leave their traces on their constitution and character.
They wear down their nerves; weaken their frame; unfit them even
for lighter studies and form but a poor prelude to domestic duties.
It is desirable that higher education should be open to women, and
girls of means and leisure should have opportunities of extending
their knowledge and deepening their refinement.[45]

In modern times the rapid growth of machinery has diminished
the demand for domestic and fireside occupations, and as a conse-
quence a large number of women and girls have perforce to look for
employment outside the range of the hearth, and to prepare themselves for this by a suitable course of study. The general impetus,
too, given in recent years to education in all its stages has resulted
in a large increase in the number of girls claiming higher education,
which is indeed a necessary qualification for positions for which
women are now considered eligible.

But the studies they engage in should be broadly those for
which their sex has aptitude and which are congenial to their tastes
and habits. They should not be set to run neck to neck with men
through an abstruse and complex programme. Whether they
obtain instruction in common with men or apart by themselves, the

male programme is an intolerable burthen for them. The programme for higher education for women should be founded on their natural tastes and on the part they are to play in the future life of the race. It should allow them breathing time, time for amusement, dress and gossip. It should consult their weaker powers, their less stable nerves, their earlier maturity, their earlier decay of mind and body. It should consult the bodily infirmities and vicissitudes peculiar to their sex. It should consult their characteristic methods of influencing the lives and opinions of the men with whom they consort. It should consult their special gift of correctness of speech, of accent, of composition. It should have in view the sphere in which they are called to move, the intimate relations in which they are destined to stand to the rising generation.

Even in the higher studies of women, the hearth, the kitchen, the infant babe, the rising brood of children at their mother's knee, the lisped prayer, the muttered hymn, the looks of uncontrolled affection, the limitless caresses of the mother, should not be wholly lost sight of. The hearth should regulate, even if remotely, their higher education. The hearth needs grace and refinement rather than hard logic; sympathy and kindness rather than recondite learning; tact rather than science; a woman with nerves and strength unimpaired rather than one whose constitution is undermined; liveliness, mirth and gaiety rather than the solemn and sombre platitudes of the class-room. Even women of wealth and leisure who can afford to get all the menial routine of woman's work done for them by subordinates and who may pass their lives in the enjoyment of comforts and luxuries, even these are not so far removed from the empire of the hearth that their higher studies can be safely directed without reference thereto. Placed though they may be in high station they influence the family for good or evil. Their example is a powerful force in building up or in destroying. The more exalted their position the more powerfully their womanly qualities when properly directed will impress themselves on the coming generation.

A woman in high station rules over an exalted hearth whose influence is of wide extent. She entertains prominent persons and is entertained by them. Her influence extends to many family circles outside her own. She is instinctively looked up to by her circle of subordinates. Her voice reaches the most distant places; her acts are imitated and commented on by many who have never looked into her face.

The education of women should aim at perfecting them in their proper character and not at effacing that character in the hope that a better may evolve. It should help to make of a female child a perfect young girl, and of the young girl a perfect woman, by developing her faculties according to their nature and preparing her for her place in our social system. It is not enough to say that woman is weaker than man. Rather should we say she is the complement of man. Men and women are formed by nature to act in concert, each supplying what the other is wanting in. They differ in the period and progress of their development and of their decline. They differ widely in tastes, habits and in their outlook on life.

The species of education that sets itself deliberately to reverse nature, to make boys and girls aim at a common standard of habits, of tastes, of intellectual development, to give them the same species of amusements, the same course of studies, to submit them to the same kind of punishment, to embellish them with the same accomplishments, to submit them to the same educational tests is to attempt to prevent the natural development of the race.[46]

Their unfitness for great physical or mental exertion, the relatively shorter period of their prime, warn us not to set tasks involving mental strain to growing girls; nor to engage them in studies requiring the drudgery of a close and protracted application; to leave them a margin for recreation and for rest. To devote the years usually set apart for education to the uprooting of the feminine qualities of girls with a view to engrafting others for which their constitution is unsuited and which the world does not require of them is to oppress and brutalise them, to blunt their minds, to rob them of their greatest gifts, to make them coarse if not insipid, vulgar if not dull. The edge of a woman's mind is fine and easily blunted; the graces and qualities in which she excels require a light soil to spring up and flourish in. They require warmth, sunshine and shelter from blighting winds.

Female education is the cultivation of such precious plants as female virtues and accomplishments in the tender soil of the physical and mental constitution of growing girls. If these plants are not brought to perfection so as to flower in due season they are apt to give place to unsightly and unprofitable weeds. Women's education should not occupy such a length of time as that of men. It should be effected with brighter touches and simpler and more sunshiny treatment. Their judgments ripen quickly, their faculties expand with extraordinary rapidity. They show a special aptitude for music, singing, recitation, poetry, living languages, painting, and if these subjects are not always sounded by them to their depths, still they will stand them in good stead with a view to the graces and accomplishments that sweeten human intercourse, adorn the home and make it a fitting cradle in which to rock the rising generation. The female accomplishments which are the most visible fruit of a well-ordered education serve to strengthen their influence with and power over men which though often abused is one of the great leverages by which human society is kept in motion.

The education of women should be less from books and papers than that of men. Books and papers are indispensable but women read in a larger book than any presented by the printer. They observe minutely and narrowly; they are quick to feel. They arrive at conclusions by a sort of intuition rather than by the slow reasoning processes of the schools. They read the hearts of men. They read each other. Quickness, sprightliness, grace, good humour, tact are expected from them rather than profound learning or intricate reasoning.

Nevertheless their education should be a real thing and no mere species of protracted amusement; nor should it consist of trivialities and the inculcation of a love of trifles and empty nothings. There is some danger that as a reaction from the tyranny of masculine curricula, such as are presented by our universities and higher schools, a shallow trivial empty course of education may become the prevailing fashion. Nothing that concerns the home and the rearing of children is trivial; nevertheless much detail may safely be left to the developed mind and instinct, to the circumstances that arise in the course of life.

Education should aim at being general. To choke it by minute details, to burthen it with crude vulgarizing knowledge, is to rob it of all of its charm and of much of its utility. A sound literary education is always in season and never fails to prove of the highest advantage to women. It serves to draw out and strengthen the finer qualities of their nature and to prepare them for wholesome reading habits in after life. It has been often asserted that women readers drag down the public taste by their selection of reading matter of inferior merit or unwholesome tendencies. It is the mind untrained in discerning the beauties of literature and unfurnished with the images presented by works of literary genius that hungers for sensationalism in fiction, crudeness in poetry, and commonplace in prose.

The literary side of female education is then of the highest moment and by no means to be sacrificed to the study of subjects of what is called practical utility. A literary education should be put before accomplishments such as music, singing and the like. It should take precedence of mathematics and physical science. It is the study most congenial to girls and the one calculated to produce the most important results. The qualities which lend a peculiar charm to women and enable them to soften the asperities of life in the family circle and wherever their influence extends are fostered and brought to maturity by a liberal course of literary study. It is of importance too that the mother's mind should be furnished, not by forced cramming but by the natural process of education, with the lofty thoughts and glowing images that the highest poetry presents if she is to exercise due influence on the minds of her children. The formulae of chemical science or the received dicta of cookery when retailed to a child in the intercourse of home life by the mother have an infinitely less inspiring effect than a quotation from a great poet or inspiring orator, a passage not memorised for purposes of retail but which learnt in the enthusiasm of youth has grown into the mind. In a well-ordered scheme of education important studies such as domestic economy and practical training in cookery, for example, will not be neglected. But a system of education for girls will scarcely deserve the name unless literature be its principal ingredient.

Gorey Library
Tel: 053 9421481
www.wexford.ie/library

Borrowed Items 27/06/2016 16:40
XXX6550

Item Title	Due Date
' Irish women at work, 1930-1960 : an oral history / Elizabeth Kiely and Mire Leane ; foreword by Mari	18/07/2016
* The everything guide to meditation for healthy living : reduce stress, improve health, and increase	18/07/2016
* Trust : mastering the four essential trusts / Iyanla Vanzant.	18/07/2016
* The happiness project, or, why I spent a year trying to sing in the morning, clean my closets, fight	18/07/2016
* The queen of the hearth / Father Patrick Dinneen ; with an introduction and notes by Philip O'Leary.	18/07/2016

ndicates items borrowed today
k you for using self service at Gorey

CHAPTER 5

Protection for Women

Women are weaker in some senses[47] than men. They are weaker physically. They are more irresolute. They fall more rapidly. They are harder to reclaim. Their fall brings on them greater punishment. They reign on the hearth, their true dominions [sic], and fulfill their duties in comparative security, but once they get outside that reign they are exposed to many dangers. A single step on the road to ruin is easily taken and one step leads to others; when ruin has been reached it is difficult or impossible to return from the abyss. Women relish what one may call excursions from the hearth. They love to go abroad to display their attractions and adornment; to seek for amusement and pleasure, as an antidote against the monotony of home life. They have to go abroad on occasion, notwithstanding the danger involved in relinquishing the sacred protection of the hearth. They recognise the danger but are not always strong enough to resist the allurements of the external world; nay the danger has a positive charm for them especially when they are young and helpless. They have a perfect right to seek amusement and recreation and to get a peep into the great world without; they have a right to meet strangers on occasion and exchange ideas with them; they may[48] sometimes explore and even seek adventure; but in order that these external activities may be exercised with due security, in order that they may return to the hearth unscathed, they require reasonable protection. They require that the hearth which they have temporarily left should extend its limits for the occasion and shield them with its protecting aegis. With protection they are strong, courageous, fearless; without it they are in danger and many of them too weak to overcome temptation. With protection they may thread their way in safety through many labyrinths of snares; without it they are in danger of losing themselves. Courage, lofty principles, good resolutions, strong determination to do what is right, all these are good and will serve them in their hour of need. Nevertheless even a slight provision of external protection often saves them where no resolution of their own would avail. External protection gives full play to their good resolutions and to what is sterling in their character. They grow up and wax strong under protection while they may[49] droop and wither without it. Judicious protection ensures them a long enjoyment of rational liberty. The absence of protection may bring on them with alarming suddenness calamities untold. Their very nature calls out for protection. The hearth which is their kingdom would not be a hearth to them if protection were absent. It is protection that creates their hearth and gives them freedom of action therein.

Protection is no bar to rational enjoyment. It adds a relish to their most cherished pleasures and amusements. It gives sanctions to these amusements under circumstances in which they might otherwise be fraught with danger. It removes fears and anxieties from their minds and allows them to give themselves more heartily to legitimate enjoyment. They require protection in all stages of life and at all points, but above all do they require it during the period of their inexperienced and impressionable youth. Young girls need protection when they go from home be it for a short or a long period; girls growing up to womanhood need protection as they are often thoughtless, confiding and inexperienced; as they

are rash and heedless; as they are often ignorant of the consequences of their acts. Grown up young women need protection as
they have too much confidence in their own strength as they have
been perhaps often disappointed and deceived and rely too much
on their experience. Young widows need protection from the very
nature of their state. Young wives need protection because of their
inexperience. Servant girls when going to and from the place of
service as well as when under the stranger's roof require all the
protection that can be given them. Girls employed in shops and
sewing rooms and in such like places have need of suitable protection;
girls who herd together in factories, girls who live in lodgings, girls
who fill government posts, girls who travel, girls who are employed
in clerical work, all require protection in varying degrees. They all
know and feel that they require it, but not all are prudent enough to
provide themselves with it; not all are strong enough to go on their
way without it; not all are humble enough to recognise its necessity
as a law of their being.

The nature of the protection required or available will vary with
circumstances. Girls are safer in pairs than when by themselves.
Young girls have protection in the companionship of a mother or a
grown-up sister. The presence of either parent or of both is a tower
of protection. The companionship of brothers is a protection. The
presence of a number of persons whether they be acquaintances or
not is a protection. The nature of the house visited, of the persons
interviewed, the seasonableness or unseasonableness of the hour
and such circumstances are to be taken account of in all schemes
for the protection of women. A deficient or imperfect protection
prevents them from enjoying rational amusements which are as the
breath of their nostrils. Extend, if I may so express it, the shade of
the hearth over them and they are safe. They can go whither they
will. They can enjoy what amusements and recreations they will.
They can turn their talents to the best account. They can walk

abroad free from anxiety and danger because they move in the atmosphere of the hearth and as it were carry around them its sacred shelter. How many girls and women have to work for their livelihood under strange roofs; to what dangers are they not exposed; how many of them are orphans; how many have neither kith nor kin; how many have no home to have recourse to when pursued by want? For such as these there is special need of protection. The hearth on which they are earning their livelihood should extend its protection to them and as far as possible take the place of the native hearth. This is the true spirit of the relations which should exist between master and servant, between employer and employée [sic]. The girl or woman employed should be afforded as a matter of course and routine a protection varying with the nature of the employment. Servant maids, for example, who live under their employer's roof should be as secure as if they dwelt with their parents; girls employed in day labour who pass the night at home should have the protection necessary for the discharge of their duties. Lodging houses in which girls have to live should be above every suspicion and as free from danger for them as home.

A girl instinctively and often passionately seeks a home even amid the most untoward surroundings. Once she has to pass from under the parental roof she is prepared to make many sacrifices to secure a home to which she can cling in the hour of stress and danger. If she be assisted and encouraged she will plant her domesticity under strange roofs, there to flourish and produce the wholesome fruit of peace and contentment. She will plant her domestic instincts in the most untoward places and in the midst of the most un-promising surroundings in the poorest lodging houses, in the very workhouses and prisons themselves. This domestic instinct rises superior to every difficulty and danger; it laughs at hardships and adversity; it cements new friendships and tears old connections asunder; it collects together the most worn and hopeless shreds of human affection, breathes upon them and gives them new life and vigour. The instinct of domesticity must be, as it were, the architect which will construct for her a protecting hearth wherever she happens to be. It is a force that must be availed of to the full. It must be fostered by parental counsel and encouragement and directed by the good will and sympathy of masters and mistresses and by the shielding care of public opinion and its development safeguarded by the strong arm of the law.

Girls so long as they remain under the parental roof should be trained in the uses of protection and should be taught to realise its necessity. The doctrine I should wish to see parents inculcating by word and example is not 'no dances, no parties, no fairs or races for our girls, for such gatherings are fraught with danger' but rather 'dances and parties and fairs and race meetings and such like amusements for our girls with reasonable frequency and in moderation, but never without adequate protection.' There are parents who are alive to the dangers of such gatherings but who solve the difficulty by forcing their daughters to abstain from them altogether instead of providing due protection for them. They feel that in the person of their daughters the honour of their house is at stake. They set too high a value on that honour to risk its being tarnished at joy-gatherings, but their solution of the problem is unjust to their daughters and is not without an element of real danger peculiar to itself. Girls who are kept away from every form of amusement, who have to forego party after party, dance after dance, which they might have enjoyed in safety by a little forethought and sympathy on the part of their parents, are apt to grow restive and to seek means of clandestinely gratifying what are in themselves but innocent tastes and instincts but to which their clandestinity may at any time give a dangerous complexion. Protection is not always uniformly easy to secure, but with foresight and sympathy on the part of parents, and cooperation on the part of friends and neighbours, it can in most cases be obtained. It is neither safe nor just to keep growing or grown girls in a state of perpetual abstinence from those innocent social amusements which add a zest to life, give point and emphasis to education, and have their place in determining their future. It is a policy, if carried out generally, of considerable danger. Violent repressions of instincts at once natural and harmless cannot fail to produce as violent reactions. The young people of both sexes are leaving the country districts and flocking to the towns or beyond the seas.[50] They seek a livelihood, but they also seek amusements and rational liberty. It may happen in the event that the amusements they attain to are immoderate and hurtful, and that the liberty put in their way is license. But there are many of them whom a judicious policy of supplying reasonable amusements under the restraint of protection would have kept at home.

In recommending a system of protection for young girls and women I am far from advocating a policy of nagging watching and suspicion. The nature and extent of protection must vary with circumstances. Different classes of society should receive different treatment. Education itself constitutes an important element in protection. Girls of means and poor girls will require different systems. But all, the rich and the poor, the educated and the ignorant, those who live at home and those who are employed among strangers, have a just claim to rational amusements and innocent recreation; their claim is based on a law of their nature which cannot be resisted or done violence to with impunity. They demand relaxation from the severe and taxing daily routine of work; they demand it as a remedy against ennui if they are not engaged in active pursuits; they demand it as an elevating and refining influence, as a means of coming into necessary contact with the great world in which they long to move in an assured and responsible sphere. They can have this just claim satisfied by the help of a system of protection which, while it permits them every rational relaxation their state of life will admit of, saves them from the many dangers that are incident to social amusements.

CHAPTER 6

Motherhood

To understand fully the position of women in the social world we should try to understand the position of a mother in the economy of the human species. With the exception of the first man and woman every individual of the human race depended or depends on a woman for his existence and development through the mazes of foetus-growth – a long and intricate process, to his birth into this world of tears and sorrow. Who can adequately describe the slow and precarious process of child-nursing, the nurture of the infant through the tedious years of helplessness and dependence, the sleepless guardianship of it through day and night, the caresses lavished on it when there is no one to witness, for it is not publicity the mother seeks but the secret gratification of her affection, the long vigil in time of sickness, the plaintive lullaby to induce sleep to visit her tender charge. How the mother's wants are forgotten, how her very soul is wrapped up in her babe! When her child weeps her heart is wrung; when a smile plays on its face her soul is thrilled with joy. A long period of care and of the closest attentions on the part of the mother must elapse before the child begins to enjoy the use of reason, but during all that time her solicitude never flags. If the time seem long to her the impatience springs from no weariness in watching over her infant charge, nor from the monotony of performing these offices which its helplessness demands, but from her desire to see expanding and coming to ripeness the God-given faculties that adorn its soul. Nor does she relax her efforts at the advent of reason. As her child grows up to man's estate her zeal and solicitude for his progress grow with him. She has no comfort, no delight in life that is not centred in his happiness. Strike him down with sickness and the world grows dark around her. Lay him in death and it is the day of doom. Bring him honour and success and her life brightens as at the dawn of paradise. Send him overseas to a distant land and her imagination calls up shrieking waters and wreckage floating on the waves.

Her mind is formed by nature to store up golden memories and lofty thoughts which she instills into his child mind as if drop by drop through a long period of nurture. Thoughts and memories pass as through an alembic and become transformed to meet nourishment for the dreams of youth and the poetry of early manhood. She rules and sways the child mind through the full compass of its inchoate passions and lays the foundation of its expansion. The rich imagination, the powerful memory, the impulsive will, the cheerful thoughts and all the sunshine of the soul expand in gradual process under her fostering care. The spirit of pathos, of compassion for human miseries, of gentleness and kindliness she has brooded over in the opening mind. No sorrow that overwhelms her offspring but she must share. No disgrace which can come upon him would cut him off from her affection. The world may frown on him, malign him, shun him, her heart goes out to him all the more intensely. He is her world for which she would surrender all. Her heart hungers for good tidings of his every enterprise. He is the loadstone of her thought. A city, a town, a continent derive their importance in her eyes from his presence. When he is absent all is dark. With his return light and brightness return too. The poorest, most desolate, most abandoned women on earth are capable in an intense degree of the sympathy, the compassion, of the maternal heart. These are feelings which accidents such as wealth and power and nobility leave unaffected. The great fact of motherhood calls forth, exercises and perfects all those virtues which warm the world and give a meaning[51] to human life and human society.

To trifle with the maternal spirit and the maternal instincts would be to commit an outrage on the human race. The minds of men and women the most eminent and independent have been moulded by the mind and heart of a woman. We speak of our mother with infinite tenderness, with yearning affection. We take even her failings in good part. We condone her weakness. She is a sacred person in our eyes. Her merest wish is law to us. The incidents of our childhood that memory calls up are for the most part associated with a mother's looks and voice and love. Take a mother's love out of human life, if that were possible, and it becomes dark and drear and desolate. When the mother is called away by death while the children are still young, they keep her image before their minds to sweeten the bitterness of affliction and lift their thoughts above the ills of life.

A mother's love is the same under whatever upheavals disturb the state, whatever changes take place in dress, fashion, customs and manners. It even accommodates itself to every climate and the habits of every people. It is equally intense in the naked negroes of the tropics and in the skin-clad denizens of the arctic regions. It knows no diversity of colour, no variety of language. It is not restricted to nobility of blood or endowments of intellect. It is planted by nature equally in the breasts of the great and the lowly, the savage and the civilised. It is capable of being refined, elevated, directed by lofty motives, strengthened by education, sanctified by religion. It may be debased, misdirected, made subservient to unworthy passions. It ennobles women and adorns human nature. It has power to turn the desolate cabin into an abode of happiness.

It sets the proudest hearts throbbing with pleasure. It robs the bed of sickness of its terrors. It is a relief in adversity, an antidote against infamy and shame. It softens the hard ways of the world with the tears of sympathy and compassion and grows strong and invincible in the hour of danger and of death. It is a mother's love that lights up the hearth with happiness, that attracts thither her offspring scattered as they may be over the wide earth, in China, in Alaska, in the forests of Bolivia, in the bush of Australasia. Its influence is unlimited by space; it is unaffected by time; it goes out as in a perennial stream to daughter and granddaughter, irrigating and refreshing the generations of the human race. Under that fostering influence grow up and flourish the virtues that sweeten life and afford consolation at its close. When we grow faint and despondent at the world's delusions, our souls are renewed by contemplating a mother's sincerity and self-sacrifice; when the world's falsehood overwhelms us, we recover ourselves by the thought of all the noble truth she has poured into our childish ears. It is the dignity of motherhood that lifts womankind so high in the scale of created beings. All the training and education of our girls should be directed to the work of adding lustre to that dignity. The mother it is that creates the home. Where she is, there is the hearth with its train of blissful memories, with its kindliness, with its protection. Her presence converts the mean hovel into a home more delightful to dwell in than a stately palace without her. The human race, both men and women, have an interest in preserving to the home all the dignity and honour which are its due. The home is a divine insti-tution without which the race of men would be a wild, promiscuous horde of beings without love or kindness or pity. In the home the mother is queen. There she can issue her commands. There she exercises her influence to the full and can turn her activities to the best account. There she is regarded with veneration and love without parallel in human life. There she gladdens her little world with the sunshine of her soul. She fills a place in the home which but for her would be for ever empty. Dethrone her, remove her from her proper sphere, send her forth to do the work destined for man, and the halo of her sovereignty grows dim; she no longer reigns; she is placed in an inferior position; her best endeavours result in failure; instead of veneration, ridicule. The work she is called upon to do is uncongenial. It is more difficult, more thankless, more unproductive than her natural work, and it leaves on her character unlovely and baneful traces. External duties which even remotely tend to draw the mother from her true empire, the hearth, are not without an element of danger.[52]

CHAPTER 7

The Fundamental School

The dignity and responsibility of motherhood in the family should belong to one who is free from external cares and wholly devoted to her domestic duties. Of these duties the primary ones are the bringing up of children. A mother should be sound and healthy in mind and body at the commencement of her married life. Her bodily and mental state at the time of her marriage should be the outcome of the healthy life and habits of body and mental discipline which girls have a right to expect in an enlightened age. From the day of her marriage till her last child is reared, nature intends that the mother should devote directly or indirectly very much[53] of her time and energy to the care and training of her children. No more serious or important work could be imagined than the work which nature has deliberately imposed on her. I need not dwell on the foetus stage of the development of the future race. It requires the utmost care and attention. It requires technical advice and often professional treatment. It is a period during which the mother should be free from severely taxing or distressing duties.

Nature is not content with committing to the mother the office of bringing forth children, but has set her over the fundamental school of the human race. As children are reared and trained, so will the future race be. Mothers have the moulding, the physical and intellectual moulding, of them in their hands and woe to them and woe to the human race if they neglect that duty. Woe to the present generation if they permit mothers to neglect it or if they force them by the stress of life to perform it in a careless and perfunctory fashion. This fundamental school embraces every form of training and rearing which the child requires. Its exigencies are so constant, so persistent, that it must be continued through the day and night, from week to week, from year to year. It admits of no holiday, no Sabbath, no vacation, no period of rest. It is one long exercise in tenderness and affection combined with prudence and firmness. Here are formed those habits, which, for good or evil, grow up with the child and mould its future life. Here the seeds of virtue may be planted with a delicate hand, and fostered with zealous care. Habits are inculcated till they become second nature. Not only sounds and gestures but even language, a full and adequate vocabulary and the ready and expert use thereof, are acquired. It is a school of rudimentary thought, of suggestion, of impressions, of the first inculcation of religious truth; a school in which the pupils grow up in the early stage in unswerving loyalty and unquestioning confidence; in which they regard their tutor with veneration and love, but withal with salutary fear; a school in which while they feel their dependence in everything; they are never in doubt as to the readiness on the part of their teacher to anticipate and supply their wants. They grow up imperceptibly in years, in body, in knowledge, in wisdom. Their minds expand in an atmosphere of sincerity and love, of reverence for past traditions, of veneration for authority, of faith and trust in God.

The young pupil finds himself in the process of being grafted on the family tree as is his natural right. The home and family, the dwelling, be it great or lowly, give him all he cares about of the world. He feels that there is a vaster world outside, but all that interests him in that world comes to his door and becomes a part of his home. It is by fully imbibing the learning and spirit of this school that he will be best fitted to go into the great world when he is of an age to take part in its work. He must take with him thither the atmosphere of this school, its healthful traditions, its love, its tenderness, its sympathy with suffering, its feeling of community of grief and gladness, its forgiveness of past offences, its hopefulness, its trust, its unquestioning loyalty, its unselfish striving for the common good. The great world outside cannot be carried on except on principles derived from this school. For it is itself an assemblage of such schools. Their spirit breathes through it, brightening it with the radiance of hope, and leavening it with the wisdom of mature age. For in this school youth and age mingle. There is the tender babe and the adult, sometimes aged, parent. There are the grandparents in the background. There is ever a mingling of the roseate optimism of youth with the sobriety of age such as occurs hourly in the vast world around us.

Whatever defects or shortcomings exist in this fundamental school will be felt through the entire human family. For the world is not otherwise engaged than in putting into practice the principles inculcated in this rudimentary stronghold of education. To taint this school is to taint the human race. The mildew, the blight in the blade, will infect the stalk, and reaching the ear cause it to issue in dust and corruption instead of wholesome grain. Thus a race of little ones brought up without the knowledge of God would blast into a godless age; children who become the constant witnesses of dishonesty and meanness, of lying, of disobedience, of turbulence, will reflect these vices in the adult stage of their growth; and the memory of their vices will pass from generation to generation. A people reared without God in the child stage can hardly escape being godless and depraved. In the course of a single generation what virtues could be blotted out, what good traditions forgotten, what depths of degradation and vice sounded, through the general deterioration of the fundamental school. When good instruction and good example are withdrawn, evil example and evil teaching are not slow to take their place, and having taken early root are difficult to eradicate.

Silently, with punctual routine, with monotonous attention to trifles, the nursery school fulfills its function throughout the day, and even into the night. There are kisses, caresses, blandishments; there are sighs and languishing looks; there are persistent and inarticulate cries; there is broken speech; there is play and fun, and laughter; there are tiny strides by tiny feet on the floor; there are pictures, wonder books, playthings, pageants; there are little meals, times of rest, elementary social intercourse; there are hopes, fears, disappointments; there is an exciting of the imagination by tales of magic, by surprising narratives of adventure in fairyland. There is the exciting of the emotion of compassion for suffering by stories of hapless knights or ladies in dateless bondage. But there is through all these scenes, through every change of the day, even into the watches of the night, the sweet and winning expression on the face of the teacher, the insinuating voice adapted to every mood of the child pupil directing the awakening intelligence to the meaning of everything that comes under observation, arousing the nascent passions in the soul, and leaving impressions that may grow fainter with the years, but some of which will never be completely effaced, calling forth one emotion after another, inculcating now patience, now courage, now sympathy, now reverence, with an insistence that the most stubborn will cannot resist, and unfolding gradually all the mysteries of the expanding mind. This process, laborious in itself, but a labour of love when carried out under the guidance of nature, is performed day by day without reward, often without praise, merely as an elementary duty whose due fulfillment is its own recompense. Imagine the same work going on under every roof in the realm every day and every hour of the day without rest or intermission, sometimes in the midst of privation and poverty, sometimes in the presence of domestic calamity, and always with the perennial freshness with which nature operates, and some idea will be formed of what it is to lay the foundations of the training of the human race.

Whatever tends to vitiate that training, whatever causes it to be neglected, inflicts serious injury on human society. Happy is the nation whose womankind are engaged without let or restriction, without external distraction, in the work of renovating the human race, and with them the face of the earth. The improvements which may be made as the result of industry directed by wise legislation in the face of the external world, the roads, the bridges, the factories, the parks, the gardens, the public buildings, the woods planted, the morasses drained, the wide tracts of land made by cultivation to blossom in summer and yield ripe[54] fruit in autumn, are but a faint reflection of the amelioration that is induced on a whole people through the more faithful discharge of her duties to her offspring by the mother. What the mother sows the nation reaps. It is the mother who moulds the nation, teaches it to think, points out to it the paths in which it should walk, fixes in its mind principles of conduct, lifts it up when it falls, supports its drooping figure, plants courage in its fainting heart.

If a generation or nation have [sic] the misfortune to lose its moral vigour and grow callous to the promptings of conscience, who but the mother can recall them to a sense of duty; a mother's gentle voice making itself heard amid the storms of passion, soothing, entreating, strengthening, lifts a depraved race from the morass into which it has sunk. The mother in touch with her own immediate circle, with children and husband, is all powerful; and the simultaneous exercise of such influence by the mothers of an entire country constitutes an irresistible force. When this force is exerted in the direction of rectitude, of clean living, of devotion to duty, of patriotic spirit, it cannot fail to lift the family and the nation high in the moral and material scale. A people who in their youth are trained to virtue will preserve national vigour and strength in the face of reverses. National health is an asset that external conquest cannot take away; national virtue blooms and gives forth its fragrance even in the midst of chains and in the depths of the most degrading servitude. 'It is woman alone' says the Talmud 'through whom God's blessings are vouchsafed to a house. She teaches the children, speeds the husband to the place of worship and instruction, welcomes him when he returns, keeps the house godly and pure, and God's blessings rest upon all these.'

The mother not only teaches the rising generation in what we have called the fundamental school; she continues the education of her children even in the adult stage. She is always an educator. Even when her children are scattered and far from her presence, her lessons reach them by letter or oral message. It may be but a word or two, but these words are brimful of meaning. They are as it were a recapitulation of the lessons that it took years to inculcate in the nursery. They are the old words, perhaps, made rich and expressive by the associations of childhood and hallowed by years of stress and trouble. The tone is altered to suit the altered circumstances, but the sweetness, the sincerity, the affection are all present, and combine to force conviction. How often has the wayward son, whose adult life has been passed in running counter to his mother's most cherished teachings, been reclaimed from evil by the maternal repetition of these teachings in concise form but informed with the sincerity and earnestness derived from years of anxiety and distress? The mother keeps on teaching her daughters during their adolescence nor do her educational exertions relax even when they are settled in marriage, even when they are mothers themselves. It is ordained by nature that the mother is the fundamental teacher of the entire human family running into several generations.

CHAPTER 8

Virgins and Widows

A large number of the female population of every country are destined to remain unmarried and thus never to attain to the dignity of wedded motherhood.[55] Yet even these will share the reflected glory of that exalted state. When a due sense of the responsibility and dignity of motherhood has permeated the entire community, the unmarried will come by their own, whether they live apart or under strangers' roofs or form a part of a brother's or sister's or parents' family. In her parents' household where the mother is all that nature and grace and civilization meant her to be, the unmarried girl will grow up full of the spirit of true womanhood. She will have an instinctive love for retirement, domestic work, and domestic amusements. She will be a living example to her sisters, nieces, cousins, of what a mother's hand can mould a daughter into. When her own mother passes away she will be a mother to the younger children, a true mother in all that concerns training and upbringing; she will not have learned in vain the lessons taught her by natural precept and example. She will sustain the traditions of the family and add new lustre to their glory by her zeal and devotedness, by her unselfishness and by the radiance of her unspotted life. A woman growing old in the service of her orphaned sisters and brothers, taking the place of a mother in their regard, endeavouring by her industry to supply all their wants, exerting herself to settle them in life, shielding them from the world's evils, and doing all this without hope of fee or reward in this life, is a noble example to her sex. Such a life of devotion and self-sacrifice is a natural, if heroic, outcome of the training of a good mother. A normal family may prosper without the aid of a heroic sacrifice, but even in the best regulated families occasions will arise which will call for un-wonted acts of self-denial and self-effacement on the part of some of the members. If the moral atmosphere of the family be main-tained in a wholesome state, as it will if the duties of family life are performed with becoming devotedness, the members will be apt to rise to the heroic level the most untoward occasion may call for; and no self-sacrifice is more touchingly heroic than when an elder daughter takes upon herself the duties of a mother and all the heavy load of a mother's responsibility as regards her sisters and brothers of a tenderer age, and continues to bear that weight during all the years of her prime and even till she is herself overtaken by old age and death is not far distant, with no thought of self, no aspiration to found a family of her own, no enjoying of the legiti-mate pleasures of external and independent life.

Great is the sacrifice made by grown-up girls who toil in the service of others in various capacities without rest or intermission during the most active years of their lives in order to sustain the falling fortunes of the home of their childhood and to brighten the declining life of their parents and contribute to the maintenance of the younger members of the family. Prompting and directing such sacrifices is the maternal instinct, which though not satisfied to its fullest extent in such women, still aims at such important ends as the preservation and welfare of the family and the perpetuation of its most sacred traditions. Sisters such as these cannot claim to be queens of the hearth in the fullest sense, but in their proper sphere they are shining ornaments of that sacred institution and bear living testimony to the fruitful character of the maternal instinct. The family which is a comprehensive institution affords a place and provides functions for a virgin element. As all girls are not destined to enter the marriage state there must be room in the family for virgins, women who forego the pleasures of matrimony and pass their lives in virgin purity. They have their place in the general economy. They toil and exert themselves for the general welfare. They interest themselves in external works of charity. Where their position and means allow it they are mothers of the poor. They organise charitable societies. They nurse the sick, bend over the pillows of the dying, and comfort the family and relations of the dead. Where there is a work of charity and self-sacrifice to be performed they are the first to undertake it, forgetful of their own interests and giving free reign to their instincts of benevolence and compassion. A mother's benevolence acts in the first place on the narrow limits of her own family; a virgin's acts on God's poor wherever they come within its range. She is their mother and their servant, be they never so numerous. They are her patrimony. She rejoices in the labour of waiting on them, of relieving their distress and of bringing comfort to their souls. But in the midst of her labours she is a shining light of innocence and purity to all the world. Did not such as she live their bright lives amongst us the world were drear and dark and comfortless.

Marriage is good and holy but the state of perpetual virginity is something more exalted still.[56] It is the fragrant and unsullied rose amid the thorns of a pleasure seeking world. It is the fairest flower in the garden of humanity. The world, weary of its feast of sensual enjoyments, turns at times to contemplate the spectacle of human beings living in its midst helping their fellow creatures to bear its burthen with patience, lifting them up out of sorrow and affliction and at the same time breathing a purer atmosphere and living a more exalted life than falls to the lot of ordinary humanity. The virgin who lives a pure wholesome life, and according to the measure of her opportunities passes her days in works of benevolence, and devotes herself to the solution of the riddle written and written over again on the face of the whole earth, the riddle of meritorious lives linked with poverty and affliction, belongs to the true army of chivalry which the Lamb has chosen as his own bodyguard.

Those women who lead unwedded lives require indeed protection and encouragement. They require sympathy and kindness from all classes, but they have chosen the better part. They can lay claim to an heritage that shall not be taken from them. Their lives are a perpetual reminder to the world that there is a purer, sublimer, holier atmosphere on its high mountains than that which it daily breathes. That there is a serenity and calm on the summit of Olympus unknown in the wind-swept plains below. These compounds of flesh and blood walk the earth with unsullied feet; they run in their joyous course with the fleetness of the fawn. The life they lead is ever directing us heavenwards by its purity and unselfishness. They are exempt from the thousand cares that infest the married state, from the responsibilities of motherhood, from the keen agony experienced at the loss of offspring, from all the anxiety that surviving children induce in a mother's breast. Their life is shielded from the pain and anguish that subjection to and companionship with a husband not rarely give rise to. The virgin has responsibilities which of her own free will she has undertaken and which she can forego at pleasure and which enable her to do works of charity and mercy on a liberal and extensive scale. She protects whole families, directs the young, gives counsel to those whose minds are wrapped in doubt; she consoles the afflicted, helps the living to bear life's burthen with equanimity, holds up the emblem of our redemption before the eyes of the dying. Though she is devoid of the protection afforded by the encircling cloister, though her day is not regulated by monastic rule, still does she use her freedom in a noble cause in doing good to others, in scattering blessings among her fellow creatures with a liberal hand. Virgins seem to have peculiar jurisdiction over the poor, the suffering, the afflicted among God's people. These are the children which God has given unto them, a complex and numerous family with a heritage of adversity but with a promise of everlasting life, a family made up of all that is bruised and broken, lost and wounded, in the natural and healthy families of the land, the class about whose welfare Christ himself seemed most concerned when on earth. It is a noble heritage of work and a bright promise of reward for which they may well forego even the privilege and blessing of wedded life.

But even when their circumstances and means will not permit them to devote themselves to external works of charity and bene- volence, and they have to toil and strain their strength to win their own precarious livelihood, they still have a mission of high import in this sordid world. They can help to keep the private family to which they belong or with which they live in touch with the noble tradition of purity of life and high ideals in the midst of a sordid world. The labour with which a poor livelihood must be eked out forms a background which will throw into clear relief the brightness of those virtues that adorn the unmarried state like a garland of flowers. What is poverty or privation to the woman whose purity of life shines out conspicuously among her compeers? Will not poverty brighten the lustre of her soul and will not privations be fresh opportunities of acquiring merit? How many a heroic virgin battles with the inconveniences and hardships of poverty and consents to live a life of privation and suffering rather than stain the whiteness of her virgin soul?

Virginity however attains its highest distinction when it is publicly consecrated to God in the religious state. The life embraced by religious women involves sacrifices of the highest order, sacrifice of home and kindred, of personal freedom, of worldly goods, of the prospects of rearing a family and enjoying the full measure of domestic life.

Great is the happiness which rewards a sacrifice like this. Theirs is a life of peace, of purity, of devotion, of security from the common cares, dangers and temptations of the world, of devotedness to the noblest ideal that a woman can aim at, the ideal of a mystic union in stainless purity with Christ the unspoiled Lamb. Women who live in the world sacrifice much for the sake of worldly ideals, for beauty, for voice, for an exalting wedlock, for political or social power, but these ideals are empty nothings when compared with what is aimed at by the virgins of Christ in the sacred cloisters of the land. Their days pass in quiet labour intermingled with prayer; every hour they are adorning their souls with heavenly grace and preparing themselves for the coming of the mystical bridegroom; their life is one long, happy, yearning vigil for his coming to whom they have consecrated themselves in time and for eternity. The labours and restraints, the pains and afflictions, the fasting and self-denial incident to their lives they bear with equanimity and even with joy as their thoughts are set on the blissful union with their beloved which will be without a shadow of discord and will endure for ever. Weak fainting nature is sustained by the promise of a glorious future; the drooping courage is cheered by hope and the soul is warmed by the rays of divine love. The consecrated virgin walks the earth like an angelic being wrapped in mortal clay, unstained by contact with it, as if endowed with wings to soar above it into the serene heights of contemplation, and gifted with a heavenly voice whose melody charms away the dangerous allurement of vice, and piercing eyes that see on the one hand the emptiness of human pleasures, and on the other can behold, as in a glass, darkly, the unchanging glories that her Divine spouse will reveal to her in all their undimmed splendour when the hour of the bridal feast has struck and she shall 'sing a new song' and 'follow the Lamb whithersoever he goeth.'[57]

Consecrated virginity, which is the fairest flower of the Christian life, was prized even by the pagans. Thus the Vestal Virgins were held in indescribable honour and reverence by the Romans. They were consecrated to Vesta about the age of eight or ten years and watched the sacred fire on her altar for a period of thirty years, after which they were free to marry. But they seldom availed themselves of this freedom. So many favours and privileges were allowed them by the people, in such honour were they held in the state of virginity, that marriage appeared poor and mean in their eyes. It was considered an outrage on religion to put a Vestal to death, and she had power under certain circumstances to spare the life of one condemned to capital punishment. A violation of chastity on the part of a Vestal was visited with punishment of unexampled severity accompanied by public mourning. If, then, even the pagans looked upon consecrated virginity as the very highest of female ideals, what must be the glory of consecrated Christian virginity? The pagan virgins were consecrated to Vesta, the Christian virgins to Christ. The pagans served thirty years in accordance with a superstitious and idolatrous rite. The Christians devote their entire lives to the service of God, are nurtured by the Body and Blood of Christ, are purified by the holy Sacrament of penance and strengthened by exercise of appealing prayer. In spite of all the disadvantages of the pagan system, the sterling character of consecrated female virginity asserted itself and the populace venerated and heaped honours on those who had the strength to mount such lofty heights and the resolution to spurn the grosser pleasures of life.

The tragic fate of Lucretia and Virginia, on which the rising minds of Rome were fed for generations were [sic] calculated to inspire the young with love for the nobility of virgin stainlessness.

A life of virgin purity was held in high esteem among the Greeks and Athene and Artemis, being virgin deities, were held in special honour, while the Parthenon, the temple dedicated to Athene Parthenos, bore testimony by its magnificence to the dignity of virgin life.

To widows, if they be childless, much of what has been said of virgins will be applicable. By persevering in the state of widowhood they will hold themselves free from the cares and trials of wedded life and can devote themselves seriously to their own sanctification and to the uplifting of others from misery and vice according to their means and capacity. Even the poorest widow by the radiance of a good example can make life brighter, vice more easily shunned, and virtue more readily embraced for a wide circle of her fellow beings. And her reward will be great. 'She who is a widow indeed, and desolate' says St. Paul, 'let her trust in God and continue in supplication and prayers night and day' (I. Timothy. 5. 5). Those, however, who are in easy circumstances, being free from family cares, can devote themselves with ardour to acts of public and private charity and thus aid in no small measure the work of restoring the shattered nerves of human society.

The widow who is also a mother is placed in a position of no ordinary difficulty and responsibility. On her shoulders is laid the care of house and family without the natural help and protection afforded by a husband and father. All that may be said of the dignity and duty of motherhood will appeal[58] to her with special force. In her circumstances the early training of her children is at once more difficult and more necessary than in the case of a mother who has a mate to cheer and advise her. Children who have lost their father are exposed to dangers of a peculiar kind and the mother's upbringing of them to be successful postulates on her part unusual vigilance and foresight. That the arduous work which becomes the duty of widowed motherhood has been successfully accomplished, in countless instances to the glory of humanity, the pages of human history abundantly attest: that it is a highly laudable and meritorious work is plainly asserted by the apostle of the Gentiles, who extols the state of widowhood above that of marriage while he vindicates to the widow the fullest liberty to enter or decline the conjugal state.

CHAPTER 9

Factories

In a commercial and industrial age like the present, the work of women and girls cannot fail to be an important asset to manufacturing and general industries. They work regularly and steadily and for low wages. They rarely combine into unions, threatening the industry with which they are connected with convulsive strikes. They are amenable to discipline. They are not in the habit of filling the newspapers with complaints of their treatment. They bear the stress of work with uncomplaining meekness, too often amid incredible discomforts and hardships. They are hurt and do not cry out; they are wounded and do not complain. Disease is sown in their veins and they return to their miserable homes charged with death. They often sink into an early grave, without protest or resistance. No agitation thunders above their mortal remains; their names are not sounded abroad as those of martyrs. The populace are not implored to avenge them. Their employers are not held up to execration. No. Other girls step into their places and succeed to their hardships and privations, till, in a similar manner, death enters their veins and they follow them to the grave. Meantime the industry flourishes. Fresh blood flows into it and soon becoming disease-smitten totters home to die.

The requirements of life are dear, but female flesh and blood are cheap. How often does it happen that the wages received by girls is [sic] insufficient to procure them wholesome food,[59] while the work they are engaged in is of an exhausting character. They complain not and then they accept the consumption or diphtheria or whatever disease overwork and insufficient nutriment combine to inflict on them with equanimity as a debt of nature, which it is idle to gainsay. They go forth in the early morning to meet the long labours of an exhausting day with cheerfulness and smiling faces, and return at night weak and nerveless and depressed, but still buoyed up by the thought that they are sustaining themselves by the labour of their hands.

How different such a life from that of work at home under the eyes and guardianship of a mother. The work may be hard at times but the daughters can rest; their day of labour is tempered with interruptions and amusements. Their food is fresh and wholesome; they are in the keeping of an indulgent mistress. They may lighten their work by songs, by gossip, by jokes and laughter. They feel that they are working for themselves, that their labour serves to enrich their own household and to strengthen its position. Domestic work is encouraged and developed under circumstances favourable to strength of brain and nerve, to filial piety and purity of life. How much more human, more Christian, more economic, is work whose center and controlling influence is the sacred shrine of the hearth, under the shielding aegis of a mother's love, than the work done in confined air or amid the noise and stench of factories and workrooms, extended over a long and exhausting day and for which the wages is [sic] barely able to keep the human machine in motion and not able at all to keep it from diseases that are certain to be its early undoing.

Many girls now employed in factories and work-rooms and in such-like places might find more congenial and more profitable work at home were domestic occupation duly encouraged and developed, while boys and men might take their places at the factories and workshops.[60] But much injury will be inflicted on the human race through the ill-treatment and hardship meted out to our womankind before such a revolution can be hoped for, and in the meantime something may be done to neutralise the hardships of the factories and to leaven them with the saving spirit of domestic life. For it is by extending the region of the hearth into the very recesses of factories where women toil that we can improve their condition and prevent their work from oppressing both body and spirit.

The hearth should extend its protection over factory workers, both on their way to and from the factory, and during the time devoted to the work itself. Protection should be afforded by the girls' parents or guardians through a sincere desire to preserve them from evil and not in a nagging and troublesome spirit. Companions on the journey to and from work, when judiciously selected from their own sex and class, afford an admirable species of protection. Other forms of protection which special occasions may call for need not be described in detail. As regards the hours of work, individual parents cannot often dictate terms to their employers; but the common opinion of many parents, expressed with determination, cannot be so easily brushed aside. Where girls work together in large numbers, parents should interest themselves in the conditions under which their daughters are employed, and take united action in vindicating for them such protection as wise and humane rules and regulations may afford and which would give them a reasonable chance of continuing their daily work without moral contamination or physical strain. Parents and guardians should learn to realise their power in this matter and to make that power felt in the cause of moral integrity and a clean hearth. If the home be the clean haven of protection for the household that nature intends it to be, then those girls who work at a distance in crowded workshops amid large numbers of female companions, and not infrequently amid male companions, will breathe the atmosphere of that home throughout their day of labour, and the parents who are charged with preserving the family traditions clean and unbroken will take effective measures to safeguard their absent children in the course of their work. They will take care the girls who go forth in the morning from a clean hearth to their allotted work for the sake of the household do not return in the evening contaminated and guilty things. The home traditions, the mother's instinct, that directs her to shield the weaker children from danger, should bring about a state of things in which girls, even away from home, are kept continually in mind of what their mother expects of them and of what course of action is in harmony with the honourable traditions of the hearth, a state of things in which they can pursue their avocations without being thrust unawares into the midst of alluring dangers.

The proprietors of factories will find it their interest to accommodate themselves to the seriously expressed wishes of the parents and guardians of their working girls, and will frame their laws and regulations to meet their wishes.

The sacred traditions of the home and the general well-being of the community demand that the moral life of girls working together in considerable numbers should be effectively shielded from contamination, but the material side of such work deserves the closest attention. The public should make their voice heard in all that concerns the working girl and try to secure for her a day of labour of reasonable length with suitable intervals for meals.[61] They should insist that the work be performed under conditions favourable to health and that its nature be such as not to overtax or overstrain her weaker nerves, and that, moreover, if possible the wages given shall be such as to lift the workers above the level of temptation and of dangerous dependence on others. Commercial concerns are, no doubt, worked on economic lines, and have to strive to hold their own in the face of keen competition, nor can we expect to see ideal conditions of labour existing in all such enterprises. Moreover, girls are often glad to get occupation even under distressing circumstances, and rather than pine in idleness are prepared to undertake work which will inevitably injure their health and even bring them to an early grave; and while the demand for employment is so pressing, employers cannot be expected to weigh down their business with expense in order to produce a state of things that would delight the heart of the philanthropist. Competition, the desire of employers to do everything at the cheapest rate and with the least amount of trouble, and to derive the maximum amount of profit from their business, even though the flesh and blood of their female workers should be severely taxed,[62] considerations such as these rule many an industrial concern and contribute their share to pressing down the lives of girls with ruinous force.

Private owners of industrial concerns are often hardhearted and tyrannical and show a disposition to grind the last farthing of profit out of the bones and flesh of their girl workers. Oppression such as this should be restrained by the force of public opinion. And to public opinion a private employer is amenable. But we live in the age of the Joint Stock Company. A large section of the public are 'owners'.[63] The multitude who own jointly industrial concerns, such as factories, change and fluctuate from day to day through the operation of sales and transfers. There is a secretary. There are directors. Board meetings are held. Dividends are provided for the shareholders. The dividend warrants look nice; they are clean. They do not smell of decaying flesh, of shriveled cheeks, of tubercular lungs. They are silent. They utter no groan; no piercing woman's cry comes from them. They suggest no vision of an early grave, of sudden sickness interrupting the course of robust health, of the drooping figure, of stunted growth, of long hours of labour in narrow, dingy, damp, ill-smelling dungeons till the worker is ready to sink through exhaustion. These bright and fragrant papers tell no tale of the wretched meals, of the straw bed, of the lonely desolate cabin that are the lot of so many female toilers. They lie on the table of the wealthy, of peers, of prelates, of judges of assize. They go to swell the bank account of respectable citizens. No one seems disposed to question their pedigree or to drag to light the story of their existence. Yet in how many instances do these innocent looking documents which their recipients pocket with feelings of satisfaction, owe their origin to the under-paid work in unhealthy surroundings of whole companies of hapless females?

The joint stock company holds its public meetings in which there is seldom heard any language but that of congratulation. They are public benefactors who deign to accept a pittance as a reward for their benevolence. As owners of an industry they are a scattered intangible crowd whom the complaints of workers never reach and who are never brought face to face with the actual state of things in the work offices. Most of them have an interest in other companies, and they feel no inclination to pry into their mode of working, the wages they pay, or the hours of labour they exact. Besides, though they be proprietors to-day, they may cease to be so to-morrow. Is it worth their while to interfere? Can they interfere? The machinery for interference is too remote, too formal, too inef-fectual, too forbidding. The warrant comes round with faultless regularity. The periodical meetings are punctual and edifying. Lofty and philanthropic principles are dealt out with unctuous grace. Proprietors come and proprietors go, but the under-paid work in unwholesome surroundings of so many girls goes on for ever. The Joint Stock system is capable of great abuse. It extends the pro-tecting arm of the law over the hidden tyranny of the workroom and the factory. It gives high sanction to starvation wages and un-sanitary hours of work. It shields sweated labour more terrible in its results than any forced from negro populations. But the system cannot be swept away in a moment, nor would it be desirable to get rid of it altogether. An effort should, however, be made to limit the abuses to which it too often gives rise. Public opinion must be invoked. Things hidden away from the general eye must be dragged to light. Oppression passing for philanthropy must be stripped of its borrowed plumes and exposed in all its nakedness.

Child labour in factories, shops and similar institutions should be discouraged by public opinion as a step to its total abolition. Most girls now leave school not later than the end of their four-teenth year; this limit should be extended to their eighteenth year. Girls who are allowed to grow up to maturity under the parental roof are the less likely to be adversely affected by the hardships and drudgery of shop and factory work. The working hours for girls in these institutions should be brought within reasonable limits and the minimum wage should at least be such as to secure wholesome and sustaining food to the workers. It is a modest minimum, but alas it soars high above what is actually paid in countless instances. A rigid system of inspection should secure that these reforms are faithfully carried out. The industrial condition which the great war is likely to create will be favourable to an amelioration of the workingwoman's lot on the lines laid down.[64]

CHAPTER 10

Authority in the Family

The bond of the family is parental authority. Without this it would be an easily separable group of human beings, kept together for a time by accidental circumstances but having no natural cohesion. The father as head of the family claims obedience from all. The mother as parent claims obedience from the children. As wife she must be obedient to her husband. Her duty in this respect is clearly laid down in the Holy Writ and is according to the natural law, nor will it be necessary here to expand the arguments that establish paternal authority. It is not suggested even by the most advanced feminist that supreme authority resides in the wife, though it may do so in particular cases. If then the chief and final authority do not reside in the husband, if the husband have no claim to obedience from the wife, that authority must reside in both husband and wife as equal partners. Now equal partnership in the authority that rules the family would be a cumbrous and even impossible arrangement. A joint decree issuing from both parents would require consultation and deliberation impracticable in the ordinary affairs of life. A decree could not be issued without agreement which could not always be easily secured. In critical conjunctures no action would be possible without agreement which may be prevented by strong differences of opinion, by strong passions, by estrangement or separation. How is the government of a family to go on when councils are divided and there is no legitimate means of obtaining unity? Are the interests of the family, and are questions vitally affecting the welfare of the offspring, to wait till the parental passions cool, and the parents have exhausted their arguments and come to an understanding? Are indecision and irresoluteness thus to cripple the family in every important undertaking? Is the spirit of divided allegiance to overthrow the household and disperse its inmates? The confidence which children naturally repose in their parents would thus be shattered. The domestic circle where peace and concord should have place would be hopelessly divided against itself. Nature has set her face against such a state of things. It cannot be pretended that there arises in the family the instinct that demands equal bi-consular authority on the part of the husband and the wife.

If there cannot be dual authority, both parties having exactly the same powers as in a joint faculty, it follows that the husband is the chief authority whom all others in the house must obey. In the every-day relations of husband and wife there are matters which intimately affect the family as a whole, and in which it often becomes necessary to take definite action and adopt a certain decisive policy. In such matters, as we have seen, dual authority is out of the question. As then not even the most extreme feminists claim for the wife supreme final authority, it must follow that this authority resides in the husband and that to him is due the obedience of the wife and of the entire family.

Ladies have been known from time to time to object to repeating the word 'obey' in the marriage service of the Church of England.[65] They refuse in other words to promise obedience to their husbands, being of opinion that no such obedience was due to him and that a promise of obedience in the conjugal state would degrade their womanhood. Allowance may be made for sentiment, for excited feeling, for a genuine mistaken spirit of honour and chivalry, though making these allowances we can understand that ladies who publicly declare their opposition to what they regard as the serfdom of matrimony may make excellent wives. The established order is more than they can resist. Their mistaken theories will not often interfere with the discharge of duties so plainly dictated by the law of nature.

The union of husband and wife is so intimate, the authority of the wife and mother is so great in the family, that it is not surprising that the word 'obedience' should be largely held in abeyance. Where there is mutual love and close companionship, where there is identity of interests and of cares, where two hearts pulse as if with a single beat, where everything that redounds to the honour or dishonour of the one is reflected in the other's life, and grief and joy, fear and hope are a common heritage, where both find their happiness in seeing each other happy, in such a state the theory of obedience need not often be insisted on. Where is the need of preaching obedience when soul clings to soul with the zeal and ardour of a devotee, when the slightest wish of each is law to the other, when the wants and desires of each are anticipated by the other, and no calamity that may befall the one can be anything but a calamity to the other, when their offspring look to them both as one power, one authority, one united tribunal?

Such is the ideal state of domestic unity and happiness and such has it ever been even among pagan peoples. In Homer's 'Odyssey,' for instance, Odysseus in gratitude to the princess Nausicaa, daughter of king Alcinous, addresses her in these words: 'May the gods grant thee all thy heart desires: a husband and a home and a mind at one with his; may they give a good gift for there is nothing mightier and nobler than when man and wife are of one heart and mind in a house, a grief to their enemies and to their friends great joy, but their own hearts know it best.'

But the current of domestic happiness will not always run smoothly. Storms will rise, and the bark that promised to go down to the seas of eternity in safety is tossed and rocked by contrary winds and in imminent danger of being submerged. In such dark hours one single voice of command must ring through the storm claiming individual obedience or all is lost. If the wrangle of dual authority be allowed to prevail nothing will save the vessel from destruction. I have shown that the voice of command is not to come from the wife; it must be the husband's voice that rises above the din of the tempest claiming obedience by all the authority of the natural, the Divine and Christian law. This authority, reposed in the husband and father, is the very binding that holds the family together. Once this binding is broken the family ceases to be a moral entity of cohesive force.

As, then, the authority of the husband is of vital importance in the household, it should be upheld no matter what the cost, and its theory should be insisted on in due season. Right-minded women easily accept the doctrine that teaches their duty of obedience to their husbands' command, and any discussion tending to cast doubt on such doctrine would be hateful to them, while those women who deny that authority found their opposition to it not on reason or religion but on the specious theory of the equality of the sexes. Moreover the intimate union that exists between husband and wife makes it desirable that the theory of the subjection of the female should not be unnecessarily or aggressively proclaimed. The wife is a companion not a menial, and the companionship is for life. No human law can dissolve it. Forced by the necessity of a given case, human law can indeed declare a separation, but on such terms only as will preclude a fresh alliance so long as death does not intervene. But though the bond is for life, and the woman is subject, and her subjection extends to the most intimate and important functions of life, the woman is no slave, no drudge, no mere nurse of another's children, no time-server looking out at stated periods for her pay and requiring to be watched in the performance of her duty. She must not be regarded as one having no rights, nothing to look forward to when old age comes to rob her of many of her attractions. She is the queen of the hearth and all that endearing title implies. Without her there is no home. If she be a mother, she lives in the hearts of her children. They are her children in the true and obvious sense and without metaphor. She is dearer to them in her old age than ever. They cherish living traditions of her. They treasure up her words. A slight offered to her is an insult to them. She labours indeed and is weighed down with responsibilities, but she labours as a mistress directing, ordering, approving, commanding. Her responsibilities are great, but they are such as nature urges her to assume, and are tempered with pleasure and happiness.

It is not expedient to paint on all occasions the theory of subjection in the most terrifying colours and present it in its most forbidding aspects to the mind of beings with so august a destiny. It will often be more salutary to remind them of the exalted nature of the state they have embraced and the relation in which they stand to the future race of men. The more they realise the importance and responsibility of their state the less likely they will be to seek for imaginary immunities from law and rule. In a well-ordered family the wife's subjection is the least onerous that can be imagined. It seems scarcely to exist, though it is very real. She holds sway over the entire household; she regulates the domestic arrangements; she has resistless power over the children. They not merely obey her voice; they love her with an ardour that only her reciprocal love can rival. The husband defers to her in all things, and it is he that in reality obeys her. Everything in the house is hers, and nothing is done without her concurrence. She is enthroned on the hearth, but her place in the hearts of her children there is none can fill. She may die young. The husband may re-marry; her successor may occupy the place in the hearth she has left vacant, but her own children will never be false to her memory. Their hearts will always be hers. The antipathy that naturally arises between her children and the stepmother, which has been known to every generation since the world began, is a proof of her undisputed sway. She is dead. What is the use of keeping up her memory and permitting it to darken the horizon and alienate the affections of the living mother? She cannot hear or see or speak; she cannot court affection; she cannot win over by caresses. Her rival is ready to coax and to flatter, but all in vain. That rival's blandishments are rejected, her displeasure defied; she never can find the key that unlocks the hearts of these children; it belongs unalienably to her who has passed to another sphere.

Great as are the privileges of the wife and mother from the nature of the case, and perfectly as these privileges are maintained in a well-regulated home, there are times and circumstances when she is ill-treated, when without any fault of hers she becomes the unprotected victim of brute unsympathetic force. If the husband is rough and cruel she is exposed to a sort of slavery at the very thought of which the mind revolts. To great heights there are corresponding depths. The exalted character of the position occupied by the queen of the hearth must have its counterpart in humiliation correspondingly bitter and in sorrow correspondingly poignant. The slavery and degradation of her position when mated to a cruel or brutal husband serve to emphasise the natural dignity of her position and afford no proof that the married state is essentially a state of servile subjection. So the existence of tyrant monarchs is no proof that the monarchical state is one of tyranny. The husband by behaving with cruelty to his wife outstrips his natural and legal rights. The legislature should provide full and speedy redress for a wife who is ill-treated or cruelly abused, but the redress of abuses is no ground for a revolt from the system which nature herself has called into being. Abuses of authority in the conjugal state, cruelties inflicted on the weaker vessel, cannot be altogether removed from human life, but the cultivation of a higher tone in family life, the insistence on the dignity and responsibility of those who are appointed to rule the household, will do much to reduce abuses of this kind to the minimum from which human nature being what it is cannot hope to be exempt. The law too has its duty. The redress to the wife for cruel abuse of the husband's authority should be full and ungrudging and within easy reach. The law cannot indeed be expected to regulate every detail of married life or domestic economy but should be prompt and decisive in cases of cruelty or gross abuse of power. [66]

CHAPTER 11

Refinement and Home Life

Women are naturally gentle, sympathetic and tender, and diffuse a refining and softening influence around them. Their good qualities shine most conspicuously in the home and in the various phases of home life and home duties. They refine and soften their brothers, whose intercourse with them is naturally intimate and continuous. Even when the girls of a family get no formal education they still have much to teach their brothers. Their refining influence extends to their more distant male relatives and friends. They bring out the soft and tender virtues of their fathers and husbands. Just as girls naturally possess a certain degree of refinement and politeness, so acquaintance with them is an education in refinement and good manners. It is an education that men need and that is seldom lost on them. The home is thus a school of politeness, of good manners, of gentleness, of sympathy, of kindness, of sweetness of temper, of forbearance, of patient suffering, of the cheerful endurance of silent sorrow. It is a school whose lessons are taught at meals, at work, at rest, at play, in the intimate intercourse of brother with sister, of father with daughter, of wife with husband, in the enduring of a common burthen of sorrow, in mourning for a common friend, in the experience of mutual joy, in adversity, in affluence, in acts of neighbourly kindness, in the relief of distress. Anger is appeased;

grief is mitigated; pity is aroused; joy is intensified; all the finer feelings of human nature are cultivated under circumstances most favourable to their growth. All that is gentle, chivalrous, sympathetic in man is brought into play without strain or effort; character is built up; the man is moulded gradually and imperceptibly; habits are formed under the influence of a caressing affection and a gentle voice of encouragement or reproof. His heart is moved even at his own fireside with the various emotions that stir him in his intercourse with the great world outside, for his teachers, his sisters, his mother, his daughters, are universal in their sympathies. There is no chord of human feeling which they leave untuned. For the home is a microcosm, a little world, and the soul and character of a mother destined by nature to educate the rising generation are as wide as human nature itself. To make the teaching as effective as nature meant it, the teachers, womankind, must keep continually under the influence of the hearth. There must be genuine family life. The girls must live a home life with its busy days, its multitudinous duties, all connected remotely or proximately with the hearth, its occasional stresses and strains, its jars and bickering, its transitory suspicions, its wealth of rumours, its hopes, its fears, its affection, its gentleness of spirit.

The social warmth of the family life and all the refining influence of its womankind cannot fail to suffer eclipse if the girls and even the mother are absent from home from early morning to late evening, whatever be the nature of the work they are engaged in. They return tired, weary and disconsolate, and have neither time nor inclination to give the home the form and colour of comfort and happiness. But these discomforts are intensified when girls and mothers of families are absent in the daytime and even at night at meetings or political gatherings, at committees or conventions.[67] While the mother is engaged in these public tasks the household duties suffer; everything goes wrong. Her servants take advantage of her absence. The children are neglected, uncleaned, uncared for. A sense of coldness and an absence of comfort and cleanliness will pervade the place; and it deserves not to be called a home. The one person who could make it worthy of that name and preserve it in its worthiness has turned her back on it, has gone to a distance from it, has become engrossed with cares and duties not at all in harmony with housekeeping or domestic life. Nor do such cares as these end with her return to her home. They accompany her thither. They become to her a continual source of anxiety. There is correspondence, interviews, investigations to be made, the newspapers to be read, visits to be received and paid. Occupations such as these require time, thought and reflection, and so engross the mind, that little energy or inclination is left for the common duties of domestic life. The centre of attraction for such women is elsewhere than in the hearth. The time they spend at home they are apt to regard as a necessary evil to be endured as best it may. The home with its countless interests is no longer uppermost in their thoughts, no longer presses on their minds with the weight of serious responsibility, no longer sets their inventive faculties at work to devise plans for its due upkeep. It is not polite to speak of domestic affairs in company or in the intervals of conversation that relieve committees. It is not in good taste to say that one fears that the children are crying at home, that the home dinner must be cold, or but ill-cooked, that the upper rooms require attention, that the family clothes have not got time to dry. No such language will be likely to escape the philanthropic lady who sits for hours at a committee table arranging the affairs of the oppressed women of Singapore or drawing up a protest against the tyranny of the Sultan[68] or even engaged in business connected with a neighbouring parish or a local town. The nursing of children is an occupation of such a nature that if it engross not the mind and all but consume the energies of the ordinary woman, it will be perfunctorily performed or greatly neglected. Other tasks, however meritorious, that are calculated to turn the mind from it or that occupy the time which is its due must be regarded as militating against family life and as impeding the due upbringing of the human race.

The children of the poor indeed have often to submit to rough treatment while their mothers are at work. They have to fast or subsist on insufficient food. They cry and are not consoled. They are half-naked and there is no one to clothe them. But the mother is without a remedy. She is forced to work and finds it impossible to combine her daily labour with the due care of her children. She does all that she can. She goes forth in the morning impelled by necessity, a mother, but with a heavy heart, as maternal love is drawing her back to her babes who are in her thoughts the livelong day; and when released in the evening she hastens to compensate them, if compensation be possible for the withdrawal of her attention. The caresses she lavishes on them are all the more tender for being delayed. Even the infant children seem to realise that the intermission was inevitable and their smile of pleasure seems a recognition that the debt of maternal affection has been discharged.

But with the mother who deliberately turns her back on her children, impelled by a call of public work, the case is different. She answers an external call to work not ordinarily done by women and for which no necessity can be pleaded. Obedience to such a call in the teeth of the maternal instinct argues obliquity of mind. Is it likely that a mother who obeys will have her child in her thoughts in absence or that she will hasten home when the committee is over to lavish caresses upon it? No. Her conduct seems governed by the principle that the nursing of children, though a necessary inconvenience, is after all of minor importance and should be so performed as to leave the mother's best energies of mind and body, her choicest leisure hours, her more deliberate purpose, free for external work to which no necessity impels her and which she undertakes as a public person. To carry on the domestic arrangement of a house in this frame of mind is to expose one's self to the danger of doing an irreparable injury to the family. The child is crying for its mother; that mother is gone to sit on a council or to attend a committee who are protesting against the severity of the punishments inflicted on sailors.[69] The household is unfed; the dinner unprepared; the poultry neglected; dirt and disorder are to be found on all sides; the old furniture is going to ruin for want of repairing; old clothes are becoming rags; roompaper is faded by the sun; the house presents in every apartment a neglected appearance, a place where comfort cannot abide and where if there be peace it is peace of a hopeless and despairing kind. Cannot the work of councils and of committees,[70] of speechmaking and political campaigning, of lecturing and of holding out-door demonstrations be carried on without enticing a mother-nurse from her home and children and domestic duties? What compensation is it to the family, and the nation, for the neglect of children, of home life, and home comforts, that women should utter their sentiments from platforms or walk in processions or attend committees of ways and means?[71]

In endeavouring to fix the attention of women on the hearth as the true sphere of their activities and refining influences, it is far from my intention to suggest that an unreasonable limit should be put to their energies in social life. Domestic life lays just claim to the interruption and relaxation of social events. Domesticity rightly understood and practiced is the best preparation for the publicity of social festivities. How often in social gatherings as hostess or guest does woman exert influences of a far-reaching character? Woman's social life is but her domestic life widened, refined and diversified on exceptional occasions. It affords her opportunities of extending her acquaintance, widening her influence, deepening her knowledge and experience, and cementing useful friendships. It affords her motives for the cultivation of those refined manners which are the charm of human intercourse. It enables her to turn to good account her education, her knowledge of the world, her powers of observation. It gives zest to her natural love of dress and fashion, of conversation, and artistic display. By its means she can edify a wider circle with those virtues she has assiduously cherished in the seclusion of the family. Social life is suitable and necessary for rich and poor alike. Nor is the relish of the poor less keen for its enjoyment because their social gatherings are not held in gilded chambers crowded with wearers of costly jewels and graced with festive splendour.

The nature and extent of the social relaxation suitable for women will depend on circumstances such as age, rank, education, disposition, health. Extremes should be avoided. Fatiguing vigils even in pleasing company cannot fail to be pernicious; social festivities that by their frequency or protracted nature impair the health or unfit the girl or woman for her ordinary duties are calculated to inflict much injury on the rising generation of women. Exercises that border on vulgarity, boisterous amusements, clamour, din are inimical to the true spirit of home life. The society of the vicious is to be shunned. The expenses incurred in gratifying the social appetite should not exceed what the family can afford, and should leave a margin for deeds of charity. Women should aim at approaching social activities in the true spirit of domestic life and leaving them with that spirit unimpaired.

CHAPTER 12

Economy Applied to Family Life

The more girls are occupied at home and the less they are employed outside the zone of parental jurisdiction, in factories or in in-door or out-door works where they herd together in large numbers where the work is severe and the hours are continuous and long, the more healthy and happy will they grow up and the more will their peculiar gifts of deftness of hand, of patience, of sympathy, of grace in action and movement, of ready tact, of devotedness, of perseverance be exercised in the service of the human race. Happy the nation whose womankind are mainly employed in beautifying the home, in preparing wholesome food for the family, in providing innocent amusement for the evenings of days of labour, in training the rising mothers in the practice of economic housekeeping. The modern world has diverged widely from that ideal nor can it be restored all at once, but the wholesome doctrine of 'back to the home' must be preached with emphasis if we desire to preserve to the human race their native force and vigour. The more home life is cherished by girls and adult women, the more the science of home-life and housekeeping will be studied and understood. It is a science not wholly based on bookkeeping, chemistry and hygiene; it has its foundations in the family grouping instincts of the human animal,[72] in its need of dress, shelter and comfort, in its warmth of feeling, in the strength of parental and filial affection, in the necessity of protection for the female, of rest and repose as a relaxation from labour for the male, in the spirit of religion that, strong and fruitful in the family, overflows its bounds and goes out into, purifies and sweetens public society, making of a whole nation one enlarged family. Reared on this foundation firm as adamant and enriched by the principles that experience, learning and scientific knowledge teach us to be applicable to the health and comfort of family life and the upbringing of children, the science of home-life and house-keeping cannot fail to prosper.

Everything that tends to build up and perpetuate family life is of importance. Who sneers at domestic economy? The practice of that science is calculated to create an interest in housekeeping and to keep families together which would else be forced to scatter. The holding together of the family is the strengthening of the state. The virtues of the family multiplied become the virtues of the state. The demoralisation that takes place in families when some of their numbers have to seek a livelihood in foreign countries, or become outcasts or are forced to pass their days in 'sweated' labour, cannot fail, if on a considerable scale, to enervate the commonwealth. In a healthy condition of the state family life flourishes, families are being constantly braced up instead of dissolving, their resources are increasing instead of being dissipated, their stability grows daily more assured. Prosperous and contented families, however, cannot long subsist unless our womankind are free and willing to devote their skill and energy to their upbuilding and preservation. Assuredly the science that teaches how the resources of the household may be best husbanded, how best enlarged, how secured against sudden cessation or diminution, deserves to be cherished by the philanthropist and the statesman. To make what might have been devoted to the luxury of the few serve the comforts of the many, to check waste, to bridle extravagance, to inculcate contentment in families of average means and of average pretentions [sic], is to school the masses in those habits which secure them in their homes in spite of the onslaught of adverse fortune.[73]

It is a remarkable circumstance that the praise of the valiant woman who is spoken of as a wife and mother in the Book of Proverbs[74] is to a large extent expressed in terms of household industry and economy:

> Who shall find a valiant woman? far and from the uttermost coasts is the price of her.
>
> The heart of her husband trusteth in her, and he shall have no need of spoils.
>
> She will render him good and not evil all the days of his life.
>
> She hath sought wool and flax, and hath wrought by the counsel of her hands.
>
> She is like the merchant's ship; she bringeth her bread from afar
>
> And she hath risen in the night and given a prey to her household, and victuals to her maidens.
>
> She hath considered a field and bought it; with the fruit of her hands she hath planted a vineyard.
>
> She hath girded her loins with strength, and hath strengthened her arm.
>
> She hath tasted and seen that her traffic is good; her lamp shall not be put out in the night.
>
> She hath put out her hand to strong things, and her fingers have taken hold of the spindle.
>
> She hath opened her hand to the needy, and stretched out her hands to the poor.
>
> She shall not fear for her house in the cold or snow, for all her domestics are clothed with double garments.

She hath made for herself clothing of tapestry; fine linen and purple is her covering.

Her husband is honourable in the gates, when he sitteth among the senators of the land.

She hath made fine linen and sold it, and delivered a girdle to the Chanannite.

Strength and beauty are her clothing, and she shall laugh in the latter day.

She hath opened her mouth to wisdom, and the law of clemency is on her tongue.

She hath looked well to the paths of her house, and hath not eaten her bread idle.

Her children rose up and called her blessed, her husband and he praised her.

Many daughters have gathered together riches; thou hast surpassed them all.

Favour is deceitful, and beauty is vain; the woman that feareth the Lord shall be praised.

Give her of the fruit of her hands and let her works praise her in the gates.

In this description the things that concern the well-being of the household, clothes, food, habits of domestic occupation, are put into prominence. The industry of the wife and mother is untiring. 'She hath risen in the night;' 'her lamp shall not be put out in the night.' And what is she engaged in? 'She hath sought wool and flax;' 'her fingers have taken hold of the spindle.' Through her foresight provision is made against the cold of winter. Her economy extends to the purchase of a field and the plantation of a vineyard. Nothing that concerns the well-being of the household is beneath her, nothing too difficult for her. When her husband sits in council she too is represented, not indeed in person, but by the work of her hands; her husband is honourable in the gates when he sitteth among the senators of the land. She does not accompany him to the senatorial meeting. Nevertheless 'she hath opened her mouth to wisdom and the law of clemency is on her tongue.' Where there is industry and a sustained effort to support and beautify the home, the practical wisdom of life will not be silent; numerous occasions will arise in which 'the law of clemency' will require to be vindicated, and as God has blessed her industry, so she remembers the indigent and the weak. 'She hath opened her hand to the needy, and stretched out her hands to the poor.' The business of a household adequately conducted touches so many interests public and private that she who sets it all in motion and sustains it must be prudent in counsel, prompt in decision, gentle in manners; she must unite the spirit of domesticity with the business spirit; she must not only make 'fine linen' but also sell it and 'deliver a girdle to the Chanaanite or merchant.' She fills the house with proofs of her industry. Her love of domesticity reveals itself on all sides; her children not only bask in the sunshine of her smile, they rejoice in the warmth and comfort of the clothing she has provided for them. Her counsels sink into their minds not merely from her authority over them, or from their reasonableness; they are also supported by the practical proof she affords of her wisdom and sincerity. Every incident of importance in the history of the family is associated with her name; she is the soul and centre of domestic life. No wonder that 'her children rose up and called her blessed, her husband and he praised her,' and when death calls her away she has the consolation of leaving blessed memories in the hearts of her children as well as living memorials of her affection for them.

The spirit of domesticity and sleepless industry so highly becoming in the wife and mother even of high rank is brought into prominence in a pagan poem of high integrity and matchless genius. In Homer's 'Odyssey,' Nausicaa, daughter of Alcinous, king of the Phaeacians, rising up early in the morning finds her mother Arete 'sitting by the hearth with the women, her handmaids, spinning yarn of sea-purple dye, but her father she met as he was going forth to the renowned kings to their council whither the noble Phaeacians had summoned him.' Yet Arete is honoured by her husband 'as no other woman in the world is honoured of all that nowadays keep home under the hand of their lords,' and 'hath ever had all worship heartily from her dear children and from her lord Alcinous and from all the folk who look on her as a goddess and greet her with reverent speech when she goes about the town.' Thus does this great poet suggest the spirit of domestic industry in the wife and mother as the very root of those qualities that win for her the love and homage of her children, the respect and worship of her lord, and the reverent esteem of the public.[75]

CHAPTER 13

The Spirit of Rivalry[76]

As women feel instinctively that they are inferior to men in certain[77] respects, so they naturally desire to ape them. They are loath to admit their inferiority in intellect, in the arts, in learning, in oratory, in poetry, in politics. This unwillingness to recognise their inferiority sometimes amounts to a passion. Girls in secondary schools and in universities are anxious to compete on equal terms with boys and young men not merely in the classrooms but in the cold and emotionless arena of the written examination. They desire identity of programme, identity of marking, promiscuity of published results. They know well that a course of studies suitable for males condemns them to years of oppressive labour. They know too that except in one or two departments of such a curriculum they cannot expect to achieve distinguished success. They know that the honours they covet, if acquired, have for them little practical value. They know that they may be called upon to resign health and vigour and the fair prospect of a long life, yet they fearlessly enter the lists in the unequal contest. Their courage is sustained by the distinctions gained by women[78] in certain departments of learning. These are the exceptions that prove the rule, but to young students in their eagerness for the fray they appear as the rule itself.

This aping spirit, mischievous in the field of education, is infinitely more mischievous in other domains. To it we must ascribe the desire of women to take upon them the duties of public life in many of its phases; become candidates for contested elections; to give vent to their eloquence on public platforms; to ply the profession of advocate, of physician, of surgeon. They hear men's praises sounded for the part they take in public life; they hear their eloquence extolled; they see them looked up to as practitioners, as rulers, as administrators, and they burn to travel in their footsteps and aim at reaching the same goal. They seem regardless of the difficulties that lie in their path, of the hopeless inequality of the contest, of the uncertainty of their success. Many are lost by the wayside, yielding to the stress of the combat, or are disabled and forced to turn aside, yet the remainder continue their march with proud step and intrepid heart. This spirit of rivalry may have on occasion some brilliant results and command our admiration. When calamities press so severely that women have to take up arms and fight for their lives, their homes, their altars, not through love of notoriety or the desire to have their names inscribed in the roll of military fame, but from sheer necessity, we rejoice that such male mettle is stored up in their feminine natures, and we glory in their courage and their prowess. We are glad, nevertheless, that occasions for such heroic outbursts but seldom arise and that there is no need to introduce the female belligerent spirit into the common walks of life. We admire the amazons of legend; we seem in imagination to follow them as they chase the wild boar or make war on the races of men; we revel in their frolic and feel our hearts thrill with emotion as we see them march to battle and to victory with bared bosoms, the right breast removed, their bows and arrows in readiness for the fray.[79]

We cherish the legend and hope that the warlike spirit which breathes through it animates our own sisters and mothers and daughters, though we shrink from contemplating occasions which may call it into action.[80] Such occasions are the last resource of outraged[81] humanity, when the crushed worm turns, when the long-suffering slave rises to the height of armed resistance and smites the hand lifted to chastise him, when the liberties of a people have been quenched in blood and degradation awaits the unresisting. We should then be proud of our mothers and sisters if they went forth to battle weak in bodily strength but thrice armed with the justice of their quarrel. We should honour them as heroines and champions of liberty though we may deplore such a conjuncture as the very spilling of nature's germens[82] and the upheaval of the established order. But we have an instinctive loathing for a plague of pseudo–Amazonian fury. We detest the race of pygmy martial women that jostle us in the streets, that make night hideous with their brawls, that violate the sacred sanctity of home life, that engage in unequal contests with men. We shrink with horror from the unsexed woman whether her outbursts have their origin in ignorance and vulgarity or whether in mellifluous tones and accurate grammar she appeals to our reason in justification of her deeds. It is in woman's power to make herself the most loathed thing on earth and great is the responsibility of those who prompt her in the beginnings of unwomanly life.

CHAPTER 14

Examples

It were easy to confirm our views of the importance of woman in the household and of the power she wields when she realises the responsibility of her position and honestly endeavours to fulfil its duties by examples drawn from every period of human history. Hosts of noble and unselfish mothers have immolated themselves in the sweet and wholesome sacrifice of maternal duty, women of spirit and talent who could win a name in the world by their attractions and their genius, who hid themselves in the bosom of their family and exerted all their power in bringing up and sending forth into the world men and women full of their own spirit and fired with enthusiasm for noble ideals. A son may prove wayward at first, but this will not daunt the noble mother who strives to win back to righteousness by prayer and by her own example her erring child, and like St. Monica may claim a repentant son by a two-fold right: the milk of her breasts and her bitter tears;[83] or again, like the mother of Louis IX,[84] she has the satisfaction of seeing the principles she inculcated take root in the heart of her son and bear fruit by a natural and unimpeded growth, or, to take an example from Roman life, like Cornelia, mother of the Gracchi, who when asked to show her jewels presented her noble sons. Women of brave and noble instincts will not consult their own immediate fame; their lives are wrapped up in their children; their glory comes to them through the victories achieved by their offspring, who in their turn will exalt their mothers. Every success attained by the children, every honour secured, every great deed accomplished, shines on the mother with reflected glory; they are so many triumphs of the principles she planted deep in the heart of her children, of the loving care with which they have been fostered. The good mother thinks not of her own fame either in life or at the hour of death. Her solicitude is altogether for the fame of her offspring. She is content to remain behind the scenes and to put the actors, fully instructed in their parts, on the world's stage. She hears the plaudits they win and her soul rejoices; she catches anxiously every note of approbation from the pit and gallery; the cheers sound as if meant for her. She feels no anxiety to advance to the front to receive in person the homage of an enthusiastic audience.

But there are occasions on which her instincts prompt her to make common cause with her offspring in open and undisguised fashion. When public infamy brands them, when they are outcasts and men and women turn from them with loathing, when their own lives are to them an intolerable burthen, then will the mother's heart yearn towards them; then will she not flinch from coming out before the world and proclaiming that these outcasts are her children. As it is not their own glory mothers seek but the glory of their children, so their instinct teaches them to take the humiliation of their children on themselves as far as lies in their power. They reproach themselves with that humiliation. It was their neglect that brought it about; by greater maternal care it could have been averted. It robs them of their jewel; their hearts had long forboded a disaster. Why were they born? Why are they mothers? The world has nothing now that can console them. They are indifferent to its opinions of them. They rush into the arena and challenge it to do its worst. What terrors can the worst a world can do have for them now that the very blossom of their being is faded and crumpled on the stem? The world may disown and recoil from their offspring, but they follow it to the prison and the gibbet; and it is on the fidelity of which this is a crowning test that the world lives.

In the holy gospels Jesus Christ states plainly the doctrine of the sanctity of wedlock which is the bond of the human family, and as he has illustrated the family life for us in the clearest manner by his own life at Nazareth, his virgin mother comes naturally before our minds as a type of the Christian mother. She lived a life of obscurity during the thirty three years her Divine Son passed on earth. Of the thirty years of the Redeemer's private life by far the greater part was spent at Nazareth. The Virgin Mother, St. Joseph and Jesus formed the family group – that sacred and secluded home. The Virgin Mother devoted herself to the work of the house and to the care of her Son. There is no record of any excursion on her part into public life, of any interference in public affairs. Her life during all these years was one of peace, of tranquility, of retirement, of domestic happiness. She was happy in ministering to the wants of her Son and spouse, in contemplating the development of her Son's humanity after the manner which is natural to boys and young men, in claiming his obedience, in listening to his conversation, in asking him questions. How her gentleness and tenderness adorned that family and overflowed to the neighbours and kinsfolk. How her sweet spirit shone through the occupations of the day and relieved the dullest hours and lightened the most laborious occupation. How she prayed, conversed, worked, prepared meals for the family, provided clothing, paid and received visits, attended to every detail of her humble home. How she retired to rest at night, in the consciousness that she had done her duty to her household, that her Son was a day nearer to the time when he was to make his great sacrifice, which was the prelude to his abiding glory. Surely domestic bliss never reached a higher level. Surely the course of family life never ran smoother. No public excitement, no showy external work, engaged the attention of the mother who found happiness in the performance of her domestic duties and her empire in the sacred recesses of the hearth. Even when her Son shone brilliantly in public life she remained in the cool shade of retirement and did not seek before others to catch a reflection of his glory. But when the same people who had hailed him as a deliverer and wonder-worker condemned him to an ignominious death and fastened him to a cross between thieves, when his friends and disciples almost all fled or hid themselves, she felt it her duty to stand firmly at the foot of the Cross and listen to the hammering of the nails and to the gentle voice of her Son pleading for his persecutors. The holy virgin in all this acted as a true woman and mother. In her, resignation, patience, self-sacrifice reached their highest level in womankind. But what Christian family is not richer and happier for her maternal devotion to duty, for her maternal self-effacement in the day of her Son's triumph, and for her heroism in making common cause with him in the hour when he passed into the shadow of a death of shame?

The Virgin Mary is thus a shining model for mothers in her spotless purity of life, in her humility, in her tenderness, in her patient devotion to domestic duty through a long period of years, in her cheerful acceptance of the lot of labour and poverty, in her self-abnegation in the hour of her Son's glory, in her public sympathy with him in the darkness of his sorrow.[85] Domestic happiness may be found in the humblest no less than in the most exalted homes. There is no haven in life securer from the stress of the world's storms than the ordered home. Be it empty and poor and bare, its nakedness, its want of material comforts, its poverty are but accidental drawbacks – not always drawbacks – that leave untouched its capacity for fostering human happiness. A mother's smile, her gentle words, her self-sacrifice in the interests of her children, her readiness to forgive, her tact, her foresight, her ceaseless labour without pay or reward, are factors in family happiness which not only are independent of wealth and luxury but even brought into more nimble play by poverty and adversity. The average family in every country have to struggle to maintain themselves, yet are the average family capable of the very highest measure of human happiness, of doing the work appointed to them, the rearing of men and women in health, in good aspirations, in virtue, in sobriety, to do the world's work in the place assigned to them, and of perpetuating the best and noblest traditions of the human race.

The life of cloistered virginal purity has attracted some of the most distinguished women in every age. Girls of genius and of surpassing force of character have been drawn to it at an age when the charms and joys of the social world are beginning to unfold themselves before them. It may be shown by countless examples that theirs was no blind attraction, no ignorant selection, no foolish launching of a frail vessel on unexplored waters, but the reasoned and deliberate choice of a pure and lofty if arduous manner of life which allured them by its enthralling beauty and to persevere in which they were prepared to bring into play, and in most cases did bring into play, all the force of characters of unwonted strength.

One recent example must suffice. Marie Françoise Thérèse, widely known as 'the Little Flower of Jesus,' has attained a world-wide reputation for sanctity and innocence of life. She was born at Alençon in the year 1873. Of the twenty four years she passed on earth some nine were spent amid the austerities of a Carmelite convent at Lisieux. This mode of life was not thrust upon her. She had yearned for it from her tenderest childhood and was at last rewarded with it for a long and anxious siege of the Religious [sic] gates. She sought to begin the monastic life at fifteen. She applied to the Superior, who objected that she must not submit herself to so rigorous a discipline before the age of twenty-one. She appealed to the bishop; she made her request of the Pope himself. She was delayed and discouraged. She grew depressed. She rallied. She renewed her assault with redoubled vigour and at length succeeded.

Her behaviour during all this time of trial and anxiety is marked by the calm dignity and self-possession that bespeak sincerity. The convent gates had yielded to her onset when she was only fifteen years old, but she entered with a fixed and unalterable purpose to live the life and die the death and be crowned with the choice favours which are the special heritage of virgins of Christ. Though she observed a rigorous code of rules, uncongenial to girls in the flush of youth, and lived secluded from the world, no moroseness brooded over her spirit; there was no bitterness in her joy, no sadness in her sorrow. She was ever cheerful and even gay. Her days were lighted at the lamp of virginal purity. Her own account of her life is a veritable prose poem. It has no trace of the querulousness that is begotten of confinement within prison bars; it is free from gloom and oppression of spirit. It rings free and clear and independent and earth-scorning and heaven-soaring like the song of the lark in mid-air. Here we meet a mind alert, perceptive and receptive, capable of close logical reasoning, a spirit seraphic in its ardour, yet intensely human, schooled in the conversation of angels yet open to human thought and sympathetic with human feeling, the imagination of a poet, the tender heart of a mother. Her life full of good works crowded into a few years, her spiritual fervour, her sincerity and joy of soul bear testimony to the genuine merit of cloistered[86] virginity. The radiant path she has trodden is a sure way to the portals of everlasting peace; happy those virgins whose disposition and character, aided by Divine grace, lead them to follow in her footsteps.

Epilogue

The hearth is the nursing ground of the young, the refuge of the aged, the haven of the tempest-tossed. It softens anger, blunts envy, inspires fortitude, fosters patience. It is an oasis in the desert of human life where the weary wayfarer finds comfort, sustenance and rest. It is the image of heaven. It is the fabled region of repose and bliss. Here the broken threads of love and friendship are made whole; here the weary spirit is refreshed.

Woman is the queen[87] that presides over this earthly paradise. She warms it with her love, softens it with her tenderness, refines it with her manners, uplifts it with her unfailing hope. Without her presence it were bleak and cheerless as a frozen wild. And oh how desolate the woman who has no home! For her the world is a barren waste: no spot of God's earth to which she can flee for refuge from pursuing evil, no spot beaming with a mother's smile or warmed by a sister's love; all is cold with the coldness of the grave.

Oh to ply one's work under the fostering protection of the hearth; to get up in the morning and plant one's feet on that sacred ground; to lay one down to rest with the mind soothed by its gaiety, its sincerity, its affection; to go out into the world fortified by its counsels and leaning on its strength and ever and anon to pant to its cover at the approach of danger; to live and labour with its music in the heart and in death to become enshrined in its hallowed traditions.

Virgin mother of the Son of God incarnate whose maternal virtues brightened the Sacred [sic] hearth at Nazareth, who wert deemed worthy to preside over the unfolding of the human powers of the Saviour of men, from infancy to youth, from youth to manhood, who didst share his retirement and poverty, who didst keep aloof in the hour of his triumph only to come forth and participate in his public humiliation, who hast lifted motherhood above the stars of heaven, who hast surpassed all women in thine incomparable virginity, who didst combine maternity with chastity, humility with queenly dignity, seclusion and poverty with joy of spirit, may thine example, aided by thine intercession, fix the attention of the rising and risen generation of women on the hearth as their true domain, the proper theatre of their labours, the very throne of their power. O shield from harm that spot of earth, to be found in every clime, at once consecrated to love, virtue, heroism, and self-sacrifice, where grow peace and contentment as native plants, whose atmosphere sweetens tribulation and robs suffering of its most envenomed pang. May thy life, o sweetest and fairest of virgins, o most devoted, most self-effacing and tenderest of mothers, allure the women of our age from the noise and glamour of public life, from tasks, however attractive, that are unsuited to their strength and at variance with their nature, to that sacred centre which thou thyself hast hallowed, where youth and age meet, where the strong are gentle and the weak fearless, the abode of faithful love and charity unfeigned.[88]

Teach them to labour in that sphere where all their strength of mind and body may be applied to congenial work, where to them is allotted the exalted duty of schooling the coming generation in truth, in virtue, in loyalty, in the faithful performance of the offices of the citizen, the patriot, the Christian. Teach them how they may go forth from that hallowed shelter armed with the panoply of modesty to overcome the world, that maternal and filial love are independent of fortune, that the hearth of the very poorest family may be made a perpetual source of happiness and peace.

O admirable Mother, though the hearth in the natural order is the foundation of domestic bliss, in the Christian family it shows to full advantage.[89] Here the Christian mother, the faith of thy divine Son illuminating her life, his grace adorning her soul, the radiance of thine example ever before her eyes, builds up her family on the model of the hearth at Nazareth. In this vestibule of heaven, the natural links that unite parents and offspring are strengthened by Divine grace; domestic afflictions are accepted as from the hand of God; and death itself is but the entrance to the perfect family of the blest where thou, o Mother, reignest by right of thy motherhood and whither Divine hope is ever leading parent and child.

O Virgin and mother, in addressing thee, and in recalling the sacred hearth of Nazareth, the scene of thy prayerful and laborious maternal life, I cannot but look back through the vista of years to another hearth whence I derived whatever force is in me to engage in life's warfare, to a mother who presided over that hearth with no thought of self; her whole mind engrossed by her offspring, who laboured through the day and in the beam from the night lamp, like the valiant women of the Proverbs, to advance their material interests, but to whom their spiritual welfare was of permanent importance, who tainted that hearth with no deed which could cause them shame, whose life, though reminding one of the austerity of the early Christians, was nevertheless aglow with gaiety and cheerfulness of spirit, whose face was radiant with maternal love, whose heart was warm and tender, from whose extended hand the poor were ever plucking gifts. She studied thy holy life; she daily meditated on its sacred mysteries; she filled her conversation with references to thy name; she loved to recount the triumphs of thine intercession. She adorned her person with badges sacred to thine honour, which she prized above precious stones. In the black tempests of tribulation that swept and swept again over her household, she only saw representations of the sorrows that darkened thy life and in which she was thought worthy to participate. Who could be her child, grow up under her fostering care, and not lisp thy renown, not bear thine image graven in the heart, not feel the spell of thy maternal love?

I think of her as she sat by the fireside as the evening shadows lengthened, her face revealing the serenity of her soul, and stroked my head and spoke in low murmurs words of encouragement and comfort whose memory makes music in my heart. I think, I dream, of her devotedness to us her children, so absolute that I can scarcely imagine one deliberate thought to occupy her mind which was not associated with concern for our welfare. Did one of her children reside in a distant city? The town or city, the country habitation where one of her children resided, became invested for her with a peculiar sacredness, and grew to be a part of her cherished geography. She adored the Divine Will in such wise that recognising its fiats in human occurrences she accepted tribulations – and she had her share – as gifts from the hand of God. One who had the happiness of sharing her hearth can realise what the love and hope and faith of a mother can do in elevating family life and making it anticipatory of heavenly bliss. She looked upon her children as heirs to God's kingdom.

I see by the light of memory her cheerful toil from morn till late in the night, assiduous, constant, but ever intermingled with holy aspirations or fervent prayer. Her domestic work she looked on as great and lofty as it resembled thine. She recognised in it her way, made sacred by the prints of thy feet, to the palace where thou reignest as queen. Domestic work, domestic life, satisfied her every ambition. Did not thy voice, thy looks, thy gesture, thy modesty, thy maternal love consecrate every scene and dignify the whole? There is no dullness, no monotony, where everything savours of heaven and of grace. Her day was consecrated to thine honour and the worship of thy divine Child.

She looked for peace and happiness within the narrow precincts of her hearth and found the peace of God. That hearth did she guard as an angel from every trace of moral corruption.[90]

Home of my childhood, hearth sacred to memories that will never die within me, how thou wert lighted up by her angelic countenance and adorned by her graces. What if the world grew dark and scowled on us? Though a tempest of tribulation threatened to overwhelm us, in thee we could find a secure haven. Wert thou not a world to us?

Notes to *The Queen of the Hearth*

1   See his column 'An Bhanntracht agus an Cogadh Mór' ('Women and the Great War'), *Leader*, 13/11/15.

2   At the bottom of the ms page beginning 'of boys and girls should therefore. . .' and ending with this paragraph, Dinneen has written: 'I speak of the soldiers ranged under the banners of all the combatant powers, as patriotism and the sense of duty are not confined to any race or nation.'

3   Dinneen refers to the House of Lords here.

4   Dinneen refers to the monarchy here.

5   I have throughout standardised Dinneen's inconsistent capitalisation of this adjective.

6   Dinneen crossed out 'a small band' here.

7   In a crossed-out version of this passage, Dinneen wrote: 'But the agitation has served the purpose of drawing attention to the position of women in modern life and earnest minds are endeavouring to discuss what is to be their status position in the new order of things, how they are to fare under a democratic rule such as is coming upon us.'

8   Dinneen crossed out 'will' here.

9   Dinneen crossed out 'radical and socialist' with regard to the legislation here.

10 Dinneen here crossed out the phrase 'These measures may contain something of good.'

11 Dinneen crossed out 'clogged' here.

12 Dinneen here crossed out 'Women's hearth without men would be equally desolate, equally unendurable. . .'

13 Dinneen crossed out 'the highest type' here.

14 Of the outdoor suffrage meetings held in the summer of 1910, Cliona Murphy writes: 'The speakers usually stood on the back of a fourwheeled lorry.

The IWFL tried to have two women speakers and one man . . . Obviously public speaking did not come naturally to the women and Margaret Cousins rehearsed open-air speaking "in a field behind our house with only an ass for my audience".' See Cliona Murphy, *The Women's Suffrage Movement and Irish Society in the Early Twentieth Century* (Philadelphia, 1989), p. 33.

15 Dinneen here crossed out 'though incapable of.'

16 Dinnen here crossed out the following lines: 'Her singing is divine; her music is heavenly. Let her but quote a little poetry her literary taste is admired. Let her refer to an author's work or a masterpiece she is credited with erudition.'

17 Dinneen here crossed out 'is at home just as if by her fireside.'

18 This sentence is crossed out in the manuscript, but the passage makes better sense if it is allowed to remain.

19 Dinneen crossed out 'a just claim' here.

20 Following this sentence Dinneen crossed out the following: 'Household work may be divided into three main sections: the care of children, the preparation of food, the furnishing and cleaning of the home.'

21 Following this sentence Dinneen crossed out 'It is not her part to wander forth from the home for the purpose of providing the money with which the food is to be purchased . . . though she very naturally indulges in the luxury of shopping either with ready money or on credit. The woman should not go out into the fields to plough or dig. She should not tend cattle on the mountainside or fields; she should not drive them to fairs or butcher them in slaughterhouses.'

22 It is of note that Dinneen here turns jury service into 'work of administration' rather than civic duty. Irish suffragists raised the question of women's right to serve on juries, but even after independence – and despite their service as both advocates and judges in the underground courts of Dáil Éireann – women continued to be prohibited from sitting on juries. See Maryann Gialanella Valiulis (ed.), 'Virtuous mothers and dutiful wives', in *Gender and Power in Irish History* (Dublin, 2009), p. 101.

23 Dinneen here crossed out the following sentence: 'Neither should women practice as physicians, surgeons or perhaps even as chemists.'

24 Dinneen crossed out 'native language' here. This seems to be the only place in this entire essay that this lifelong Irish language activist refers even indirectly to that language.

25 This is the one word in Dinneen's handwriting about which I am not entirely certain. If, however, we assume Dinneen neglected to cross the second 't' in this word, the reading becomes clear. The word is used again a few lines below, where it is written a bit more legibly.

26 Dinneen crossed out 'a degree of happiness' here.

27 Dinneen had originally added here 'of eighteen, let us say.'

28 See his column 'Oideachas do Ghearrachailidhibh Scoile' ('Education for Schoolgirls'), *Leader*, 2/9/18.

29 Dinneen's unpublished essay on his mother (NLI MS. 8628) focuses on her extraordinary piety: 'After eating, she took on the day's work in earnest and that work was prayers, prayers throughout the whole day and into the middle of the night' ('Tar éis proinn do chaitheamh is eadh do luigh sí ar obair an lae i gceart agus do b'é an obair sin ná urnaighthe, urnaighthe ar feadh an lae ar fad agus go lár na hoidhche amach'). Indeed, he states that she often continued 'saying her prayers intensely and fervently until the cock's crow or daybreak, paying attention to nothing going on around her, just revealing her mind to God' ('go glaodhach an choiligh nó go breacadh lae ag rádh a hurnaighthe go dian dúthrachtach gan suim aice dá cur i n-aoinni bheadh ar siubhal 'na timcheall acht í ag nochtadh a haigne chun Dé'). She attended Mass twice on Sundays when she could, felt 'envy' ('formad') for saints and nuns, and experienced 'a kind of joy . . . along with the sorrow when sinless young children would die' ('saghas áthais . . . i dteannta an bhróin nuair a gheibheadh páistidhe óga gan pheacadh bás'). It is perhaps no wonder that Dinneen's biographers could write: 'Like many other people who share a house with a "saint", Matthew Dinneen [Dinneen's father] was not all that pleased by his wife's constant practice of piety' ('Dála go leor daoine eile a raibh "naomh" in aon teach leo, ní mó ná sásta a bhíodh Maitiú Ó Duinnín le síor-chleachtadh na cráifeachta ag a bhean'). These biographers write of the influence of his upbringing on Dinneen himself: 'More than anything else, one will see the appropriate piety and the excessive piety that surrounded him in conflict so that at last they turned into a lack of piety' ('Thar aoinní eile chífear an cheartchráifeacht agus an róchráifeacht a bhí timpeall air ag coimhlint le chéile go ndearna neamhchráifeadht díobh fá dheireadh'). See Proinsias Ó Conluain and Donncha Ó Céileachair, *An Duinníneach: An tAthair Pádraig Ó Duinnín, a shaol, a shaothar agus an ré inar mhair sé* (*Dinneen: Father Patrick Dinneen, his life, his work and the period in which he lived*) (Baile Átha Cliath, 1958), p. 38, p. 56.

30 Following this sentence in the manuscript Dinneen crossed out 'The evils and dangers of co-education are many and serious.'

31 Dinneen crossed out 'Coeducation is fundamentally objectionable. . .'

32 Dinneen crossed out 'herd in droves' here.

33 Dinneen crossed out 'many' here.

34 Dinneen crossed out 'on the great majority of subjects' here.

35 Dinneen crossed out 'great majority' here.

36 Dinneen crossed out 'generally' here.

37 'Cerebrasthenia' refers to the nervous incapacity of the brain.

38 Dinneen crossed out 'outside of a reasonable course of modern literature' here.

39 Dinneen himself was, of course, a mathematician, studying the subject at University College Dublin and serving for a year after his graduation as assistant to John Casey, the Professor of Mathematics at UCD. He then taught maths at Mungaret College in Limerick and St Stanislaus College in Tullabeg. See Ó Conluain and Ó Céileachair, *An Duinníneach*, pp 90–5. As in other areas in this essay, Dinneen was fighting a rearguard action here, as by the turn of the twentieth century the number of girls studying maths – and science – was increasing as girls prepared themselves for the examinations of the Royal University.

40 Dinneen took a great interest in the classics. He published a good number of essays on Greek and Latin literature in his column in *The Leader*, more than 20 of them in 1926. He collected these essays in *Aistí ar Litridheacht Ghréigise is Laidne* (*Essays on Greek and Latin Literature*) in 1929. Indeed he could go so far as to say: 'It is not a good thing for the students who take on the task of learning Latin and Greek to take on many other educational subjects. Those two languages are almost enough as educational material without going beyond them. The person who is educated in Latin and Greek is a learned man with a good upbringing' (Ní maith an rud do sna dáltaibh a thógann foghluim na Laidne is na Gréigise mar chúram ortha féin an iomad d'adhbharaibh oideachais eile do tharraing chúcha. Is beag ná gur leor an dá theangain sin mar adhbhar oideachais agus gan dul thársta. Fear léigheanta go mbíonn tabhairt suas maith air is eadh an té atá oilte ar an Laidin agus ar an nGréigis) (*Leader*, 14/8/20). Interestingly enough, Brian Harrison notes that English anti-suffragists were often classical enthusiasts. See Brian Harrison, *Separate Spheres: The Opposition to Women's Suffrage in Britain* (London, 1978), p. 100. As was true with regard to mathematics, Irish girls at this time were increasingly studying Latin to prepare for the examinations of the Royal University, with a girl from the Loreto Convent winning a gold medal for first place in all Ireland for classics in 1896. See Anne V. O'Connor, 'The revolution in girls' secondary education, 1860–1910', in *Girls Don't Do Honours: Irish Women in Education in the 19th and 20th Centuries*, Mary Cullen (ed.) (n.p. [Dublin], 1987), pp 31–54; and Eibhlín Breathnach, 'Charting new waters: women's experience in higher education, 1879–1908,' in *Girls Don't Do Honours*, pp 55–78.

41 Dinneen crossed out 'they are failures' here.

42 Dinneen crossed out 'far behind' here.

43 Dinneen crossed out 'up to a certain point' here.

44 Dinneen here crossed out the following sentence: 'To speak generally, and leave a suitable margin for exceptional cases, the minds of girls are not suited for abstract studies. When they talk classics or high criticism or progressive science they either expose themselves to ridicule or leap to generalities which are accepted in conversation through politeness or good breeding.'

45 Apparently Dinneen felt that only 'girls of means and leisure' should have such opportunities.

46 Dinneen here crossed out 'is to declare war on human nature and an attempt to prevent the natural development of the race.'

47 Dinneen here crossed out 'in many senses of the word.'

48 Dinneen crossed out 'have a right to' here.

49 Dinneen crossed out 'would' here.

50 The depopulation of rural areas and emigration from Ireland were major areas of concern for many in the cultural revival.

51 This word is crossed out in the manuscript but is obviously required here.

52 Dinneen here crossed out 'should be regarded with suspicion.' He then ended this section with the following sentence: 'One external duty follows another. The habit of wandering abroad grows and is difficult to eradicate. External duties bring with them cares and burthens. . .' Note the similarities between Dinneen's thinking here and Article 41.2. 1°and 2° of *Bunreacht na hÉireann* (1937): '1° In particular, the State recognises that by her life within the home, woman gives to the State a support without which the common good cannot be achieved. 2° The State shall, therefore, endeavour to ensure that mothers shall not be obliged by economic necessity to engage in labour to the neglect of their duties in the home.'

53 Dinneen crossed out 'practically all' here.

54 In the manuscript Dinneen has written at this point 'here a page of 1st draft is missing.'

55 In 1891, there were 225,000 women in domestic employment in Ireland, with another 139,000 single women caring for parents or brothers. See Mary E. Daly, *Social and Economic History of Ireland Since 1800* (Dublin, 1981), p. 106.

56 Dinneen here reflects Catholic teaching going back to I. Corinthians. 7.

57 Dinneen is quoting from Revelations. 14.

58 'Apply' would seem to make more sense here.

59 Dinneen took an interest in the nutrition of the poor, particularly of poor working women. See, for example, his columns in *The Leader* for 10/12/10; 20/12/12; 1/3, 12/4, and 3/5/13.

60 Apparently he was not troubled by the idea of men and boys working in such dreadful conditions.

61 Predictably enough, in the following discussion Dinneen sees no role for trades unions in the provision of such improved conditions.

62 Dinneen crossed out 'strained beyond endurance' here.

63 Dinneen himself owned stocks in several companies, including the Great Southern and Western Railway, Arnott's department store, *The Freeman's Journal*, and the Marconi Wireless Company. See Ó Conluain and Ó Céileachair, *An Duinníneach*, pp 249–50.

64 Dinneen's views are surprisingly progressive here, although again he seems to ignore the plight of the working man.

65 Dinneen may have been aware that the Sheehy-Skeffingtons had omitted the word 'obey' from their wedding vows. Had he known of it he would have been shocked by some feminists' equation of marriage with parasitism or prostitution. See Dana Hearne, *The Development of Irish Feminist Thought: A Critical Analysis of The Irish Citizen, 1912–1920* (Ann Arbor, 1998), p. 98, pp 164–5.

66 Dinneen is here obviously thinking about the abuse of women by drunken husbands. In his previously cited undated ms. on temperance, he wrote: 'It is remarkable that a house in which one or more drunkards reside generally presents a squalid, tumble-down appearance... Social family life has received a severe wound, domestic affection is well-nigh shattered, suspicion, doubt, distrust fill the minds of parents towards their children and children towards their parents. . . Discord becomes rife, bickerings, quarrels, mutual recriminations are of daily occurrence. A curse has lighted on that house, whose fruits are gloom in every face, the sinister light of suspicion in every eye, sadness in every heart...'

67 Dinneen originally ended this sentence 'and return at night to the home where the comforts are few and where everything is in disorder.' The mother in his anti-suffrage play provided here in the appendix is guilty of such behaviour.

68 Dinneen crossed out 'Czar of all the Russias' here.

69 Dinneen originally included 'a jury' as among her possible destinations.

70 Dinneen originally included 'juries' here.

71 Dinneen originally ended this paragraph with the sentence 'These tasks can be performed and better performed by others, by men, while no one can fulfill the place of a mother...'

72 Dinneen gives an unexpected nod to Darwin here.

73 Dinneen originally ended this sentence with the words 'war and famine.'

74 Dinneen quotes here from the Catholic Douay-Rheims version of the Bible.

75 See the three short chapters on Homer in Dinneen's *Aistí ar Litridheacht Ghréigise is Laidne*, (Baile Átha Cliath, 1929), pp 7–18.

76 This section was originally titled 'The Woman's Viewpoint'.

77 Dinneen crossed out 'many' here.

78 Dinneen crossed out 'by a few women' here.

79 Dinneen added the following passage in pencil here and then crossed it all out: 'but we instinctively loathe a plague of pseudo-Amazonian fury. We detest the race of false pygmy martial women that jostle us in the street, that make night hideous with their brawls, that violate the sacred serenity of home life, that engage in unequal contests with men. We shrink with horror from the unsexed woman whether her outbursts have their origin in ignorance and vulgarity or whether in mellifluous tones and accurate grammar she appeals to our reason to justify her deeds. It is alas in woman's power to make herself the most loathed thing on earth, and great is the responsibility of those who prompt her in the beginning of unwomanly life.' He then used a slightly reworded version of this passage to conclude this section.

80 See his essay 'Ban-Churadh Ghaedhealach' ('An Irish female warrior'), in *Aistí ar Litridheacht Ghréigise is Laidne*, pp 147–50.

81 Dinneen crossed out 'suffering' here.

82 *OED* defines this word as 'rudiment of an organism, a germ' and states that it is 'now only *fig.*'

83 St Monica was the mother of St Augustine.

84 Dinneen crossed out 'Louis XI' here.

85 One wonders what Dinneen would have thought when in 1915 Catherine Mahon of the Irish Catholic Women's Suffrage Society, wrote: 'In no country is there such devotion to the Mother of God as in Ireland. We hope to enlist Irishwomen to work for her honour, and helped by her good counsel, to establish in Ireland social conditions worthy of a Christian land' (Mahon, quoted by Murphy, *The Women's Suffrage Movement*, p. 142).

86 Dinneen crossed out 'heroic' here.

87 Dinneen crossed out 'guardian angel' here.

88 Everything after this point is filed with the epilogue in the manuscript but has 'Introductory' written in the left margin where Dinneen indicated the relevant section title on each page. The context makes clear that this material belongs here as the conclusion of the epilogue.

89 Dinneen here crossed out 'it is only in the Christian family it shows to full advantage.'

90 In his unpublished essay on his mother, Dinneen wrote of her profound devotion to the Virgin Mary, who was 'the guiding force of her life and her solace in this world' (treoir a beathadh agus a sólás san tsaoghal so) and of how she imagined Mary 'managing the heavenly Home' ('ag riaradh an Áruis neamhdha').

Appendix

PORTION OF A PLAY, IN ENGLISH[1]
(NLI MS. 8623, folder 19)

Martha	mother, suffragette
Una	daughter, suffragette, in love with Tatterdale
Henrietta	daughter, non-suffragette, in love with Colman
Alphonsus	father, non-suffragette
Simon	son
Robrich	itinerant speaker etc., socialist, in love with young Henrietta
Tatterdale	itinerant speaker etc., socialist, in love with Una
Phyllis	spinster, suffragette
Artemis	spinster, suffragette
Julia	spinster, suffragette
Colman	M. P. etc., in love with Henrietta
Kitty	housemaid
Maud	housemaid

SCENE I
Alphonsus' house
Alphonsus, Henrietta, Simon, Kitty

Alphonsus:	Henrietta, where is thy mother?
Henrietta:	She is gone to the meeting, father.
Alphonsus:	What meeting?
Henrietta:	A meeting of the Association for Women's Rights.
Alphonsus:	Association for Women's Rights! We are sick of that Association. Who went with her?
Henrietta:	No one but Una.
Alphonsus:	Una is attending a good school. She will soon be as learned as the teacher. When will they return?
Henrietta:	I cannot say, father. Mother said she might come by the latest train if the business were not too heavy. Otherwise, they would remain over night.
Alphonsus:	Remain over night? Are you serious?
Henrietta:	So she said, father. It is getting late now. They will hardly come tonight.
Alphonsus:	Have the children been to school to-day?
Henrietta:	No, father. Mother took away the keys and I could not get them their school clothes. The cattle and pigs too could not be fed as we had not the keys of the store-room. I had to let a large package of goods go from the door as the porter who brought them would not leave them without the money.
Alphonsus:	You had no money?
Henrietta:	Not a farthing. Mother said she would not have enough for the day's expenses in town and so she took all that was in the house.
Alphonsus:	Oh, oh. This is dreadful. Are there any letters?

Henrietta:	Yes, but they look like bills. (She hands him some letters.)
Alphonsus:	(opening the letters) What is this? 'To Henage and Co. 5000 copies pamphlet "Women and Social Progress" by Mrs Alphonsus. £50. Prompt payment desired.' Dear me. (opens another letter, reads) 'Sir, I beg to inform you that Mrs Alphonsus' subscription of £10 to the Women's Rights of Labour Society is now due. An early remittance will oblige yours sincerely, Isolde Chessworth, Hon. Sec.'
Henrietta:	Mother speaks highly of this society.
Alphonsus:	I know she does, but who is going to give her £10 for it? We are robbed clean. (opens another letter and reads) 'To Trumpery, Barker and Co. Mrs Alphonsus. 80 dresses for children's Labour procession. £60.10.6.' Oh dear, oh dear, is this to go on for ever? (opens another letter and reads) 'Sir. The bill which we sent some months ago to Mrs Alphonsus, being £32.8.6, for goods bought of us by Mrs Alphonsus and her daughter Una in connection with the meeting and procession in favour of women's rights, is still unpaid. We beg to say that unless there be a settlement of same within a month from this date we will put the matter into the hands of our solicitors. Ys faithfully, Skinner and Malone.' Meeting and procession in favour of women's rights! What on earth have I got to do with women's rights?
Henrietta:	When mother is here you play a different tune.
Alphonsus:	Now Henrietta, do not tease me. I really can't stand this. (opens another letter and reads) What! another

bill? This time from a Press Agency for special reports of meetings. (throws down the letter) I cannot go on with this sort of thing. We are robbed and must become bankrupt. This is what we have gained by women's rights. The house is neglected. The children are neglected. Everything is upside down and expenses daily incurred for traveling and for the upkeep of committees. We are robbed and no mistake.

Henrietta: There are several letters awaiting mother. I am sure they are equally interesting.

Alphonsus: Oh! I dare not look at them. But I tremble for our household.

Enter Martha and Una

Alphonsus: Martha my dear, you are welcome home. Welcome, Una my darling. How have you fared?

Martha: (sits down panting): Is dinner ready? We are faint with hunger. Oh! Oh! It was an exhausting day. Oh, the police. They are a band of inhuman cut-throats. They are unfit for any civilised society. Oh, the villains, the scoundrels.

Una: We taught them a lesson, mother, they will not soon forget.

Martha: Oh, the villains. They are only just acting as their masters order them. They show fair play; they consider women's rights and privileges. They look to the physically weak, the brutes.

Alphonsus: My dear, what is the matter? What did they do?

Martha : They did what they have ever been doing and what they will continue to do till the tyranny of men over women is overthrown. They sought to break up our meeting and had the savagery to beat some of our speakers.

Alphonsus: To beat them did you say?

Una: Yes, they did beat me. I have a pain in my head from a blow given me by a cowardly beast of a peeler. But we were even with them.

Martha: What is the government going to do with this pack of peelers? They are fitting tools in their masters' hands. No wonder they war on defenceless women, seeing that not a single woman's voice is raised in Parliament against them.

Alphonsus: My dear, things will not continue in this way. Women's voice must be heard in Parliament and that before long.

Una: Well spoken, Papa.

Henrietta: What, are you turned women's righter, father?

Una: Henrietta, how dare you interfere in papa's affairs?

Martha: It is that troublesome girl again. Go to her. Henrietta, you much need instruction and must have it. I will soon put you in good hands.

Henrietta: Thanks, mother. I trust you will not have me made as forward as Una.

Una: Impertinent girl. You are a libel on your noble sex. Is that our thanks for endeavouring to emancipate you?

Martha: She is young, Una. We must get her taken in hand at once.

Henrietta: Thank you, mother. There are some letters here for you. But you are tired after the day's proceedings.

Martha:	I can't be bored with letters now. (taking the letters and thrusting them into her pocket) How people will write, write, forgetting how busy one is.
Henrietta:	But mother, some of them may be bills and so require immediate attention.
Martha:	Bills, bills, really, child, you are too silly. The great question of women's rights in this realm and in the universe itself is demanding the attention of all thoughtful people. It is occupying every moment of our working day. It is disturbing our repose by night, and you are so silly as to think I will trouble myself with bills to the exclusion of my natural repose.
Alphonsus:	My Martha is right, Henrietta. This is not the time to trouble her with such things. Martha my love, when you have a quiet moment kindly look after some bills that reached me to day, bills for debts incurred by you in your most laudable propaganda.
Martha:	Now Alphonsus, don't be childish. What huxter could be so mean as to persecute me like this in the midst of my labours and to send the bill to you? Gracious heavens, is this the idea they have of women's power and position? The sordid dastards, they must be taught a lesson. I will never pay a farthing of any bill sent to you, Alphonsus. Mind that. It is low. I say it is disgraceful to treat a woman in that way. When we get power we will teach these folk a lesson.
Alphonsus:	So we will, my dear, but if in the meantime we become bankrupt?
Martha:	Bankrupt! Fiddlesticks! How much afraid you are, Alphonsus, of the terrors which an iniquitous law

holds over your head, a law your sex have made bankrupt. Let it be imprisonment for debt. How delightful. 'Mrs Martha Alphonsus has been imprisoned for debts incurred in the Women's Rights Campaign. Her heroic daughter Una has accompanied her to jail.' This paragraph would be nice reading in the press and a nice point to heckle your unscrupulous ministers on in Parliament. It would advance the cause of woman's emancipation more than all our speeches. A day in prison would be a recreation compared to the day we have just passed. Bankruptcy, the prison, anything rather than yield to these wretches.

Alphonsus: Be calm, my dear, how could you think of going to prison and leave your dear children uncared for?

Martha: What my dear children want most is the vivifying example of those who fight for the freedom of our trampled on and outraged sex. That example I can give them in prison.

Una: So can I, mother, and it is my wish to do so at the first opportunity.

Alphonsus: We cannot do without you, Una. You must not go to prison. Better we should all go than separate in such fashion.

Martha: Una is safe. She is walking in the path of truth. It is Henrietta that has to be looked to. It is a misfortune that one so degenerate as she should have sprung from me and should abide under my roof. I must see that she is properly taken in hand and instructed in the truth.

1   Dinneen may have been inspired to start this play in response to short suffrage propaganda plays by both British and Irish writers. Examples of such plays by Irish authors include *Toilers* by a Miss Day (*IC*, 4/10/13), *Candidates* by Francis Cruise O'Brien, staged by amateurs on the same programme as Annie J. W. Lloyd's *A Question of Honour* at the Abbey Theatre in March 1914 (*IC*, 28/3 and 4/4/14), and *The Prodigal Daughter* by Francis Sheehy-Skeffington. This last was published in *IC*, 7/11/14, and as a penny pamphlet the following year (*IC*, 26/6/15). Dinneen's reason for abandoning the play should be obvious. I have had to add a good deal of punctuation to his script. The text is published through the courtesy of the National Library of Ireland.